Nepali
phrasebook

Mary-Jo O'Rourke
with
Bimal Shrestha

D0939161

Nepali Phrasebook
  2nd edition

Published by
  Lonely Planet Publications Pty Ltd (A.C.N. 005 607 983)
  PO Box 617, Hawthorn, Vic 3122, Australia
  Lonely Planet Publications, Inc
  PO Box 2001A, Berkeley, CA 94702, USA

Printed by
  Colorcraft Ltd, Hong Kong

Published
  March 1992

About This Book
This edition was written by Mary-Jo O'Rourke, with assistance from Bimal Shrestha. The 1st edition was written by Margit Meinhold, with the assistance of Prakash A Raj. Sally Steward edited the book and Greg Herriman was responsible for cover, illustrations and design.

National Library of Australia Cataloguing in Publication Data

O'Rourke, Mary-Jo
  Nepali Phrasebook

  ISBN 0 86442 145 1

  1. Nepali language – Conversation and phrase-books – English.
  I. Meinhold, Margit. Nepal phrasebook. II. Title. (Series: Language survival kit).

495.183421
© Copyright Lonely Planet 1992

Contents

INTRODUCTION 5

PRONUNCIATION 7

Vowels 7   Word Stress 10
Consonants 8

GRAMMAR 12

Word Order 12   Verbs 17
Nouns 12   Questions 27
Demonstratives 13   Prepositions 28
Adjectives 14   Conjunctions 28
Pronouns 14   'Other' 28

GREETINGS & CIVILITIES 29

Greetings 29   Attracting Someone's
Please & Thank You 30   Attention 30
Hajur 30   Other Civilities 31

SMALL TALK 32

Help! 32   Age 36
Top 10 Useful Phrases 32   Occupations 37
Meeting People 33   Religion 38
Forms of Address 33   Yes & No 38
Other Family Terms 34   Feelings 39
Nationalities 35   Some Useful Phrases 40

GETTING AROUND 41

Finding Your Way 41   Bus 43
Directions 41   Taxi/Autorickshaw 45
Getting Around 42   Instructions 45
Buying Tickets 43   Some Useful Words 45

ACCOMMODATION 47

Finding Accommodation ...47   Some Useful Words 52
At the Hotel 48

AROUND TOWN 54

At the Post Office	54	At the Bank	55
Telephone	55	Sightseeing	56

TREKKING 58

Hiring Porters	59	Birds	66
Asking Directions	60	Insects	67
Along the Way	62	Plants	67
Weather	64	Some Useful Phrases	68
Animals	65	Some Useful Words	68

FOOD 70

At the Restaurant	71	Nuts	75
Meat	72	Herbs, Spices &	
Vegetables	72	Other Condiments	76
Cereals & Legumes	73	Drinks	77
Fruit	74	Some Useful Words	77
Dairy Products	75	Table Articles	78
Bread	75	Some Useful Phrases	78

SHOPPING 79

Bargaining	80	Photography	85
Souvenirs	81	Smoking	85
Clothing	82	Weights & Measures	86
Colours	83	Size & Quantity	86
Toiletries	84	Some Useful Phrases	87
Stationery &		Some Useful Words	88
Publications	84		

HEALTH 89

Complaints	90	Body Parts	93
Some Useful Phrases	92	Some Useful Words	94

TIME, DATES & FESTIVALS 96

Telling the Time	96	Some Useful Words	99
Days of the Week	97	Some Useful Phrases	100
The Nepalese Calendar	97	Festivals	100

NUMBERS 112

Cardinal Numbers	114	Ordinal Numbers	116

VOCABULARY 117

EMERGENCIES 141

Introduction

Nepal has become very popular with travellers from all over the world since it opened its long-closed doors to foreigners in 1951. Most Nepalese you are likely to meet will speak some English, especially in urban and popular tourist areas. However, as a traveller you'll find that life in a foreign country is a lot easier and more interesting if you try to learn a little of the language. Even if you're not fluent, being able to communicate on a basic level will help to narrow the cultural gap and so deepen your experience of a different society.

Trekking is one of the most popular activities in Nepal, and if you want to move away from the main tourist centres it can be difficult to find local people who speak more than rudimentary English, as many hill villages still lack even basic educational facilities.

Nepali belongs to the Indo-European language family, closely related to Hindi, and distantly to English, French and German. Nepali is not only the language of Nepal, but is widely spoken in Sikkim and Darjeeling in India, parts of Tibet and Bhutan. Altogether it is spoken by some 25 million people. Peace Corps volunteers and other long-term foreign residents of Nepal are among the many non-native speakers of Nepali, and it is also a second language for about 40% of the population. In this ethnically heterogenous country of 19 million people and more than 22 indigenous languages, Nepali, as the national language, provides a lingua franca for the many different ethnic groups, and acts as a unifying force among its diverse people.

Nepali is written in the Devanagari script, a writing form also used for Hindi, and for Sanskrit, the parent of both languages.

Nepali has 67 characters and, unlike English, most of them have only one pronunciation. Likewise, most Nepali sounds have only one spelling. This almost one-to-one correspondence between sounds and letters means that spelling in Nepali is much more straightforward than in English!

However, Nepali does have a number of dialects, or different accents. This phrasebook uses the standard form, which is understood throughout most of the language area.

There is also a number of fairly significant differences between everyday spoken Nepali and the more formal written language. However, the information in this book is presented in the informal spoken style, which is all that travellers will find necessary. Nepali is a fairly easy language to learn, and this phrasebook concentrates on conversational Nepali, not the finer points of grammar or the script. Particular attention has been given to situations where English is less likely to be spoken. All you need to make learning Nepali enjoyable are a few Nepali companions to practise with, and that will prove impossible to avoid in friendly Nepal. So, arm yourself with a few phrases from this book, and be prepared for some fascinating encounters.

Good luck in your travels and *namaste!*

Abbreviations Used in This Book

f – feminine
inf – informal
m – masculine
n – noun
pl – plural
sg – singular
v – verb

Pronunciation

Most of the vowel and consonant sounds of English are also found in Nepali. There are a few consonants with no English equivalent, but these are not very difficult to learn.

Vowels

There are six vowels and two vowel combinations (diphthongs) in Nepali, and most of these also occur as nasal vowels, making 15 in all. The nasals are similar to those of French, with the airstream coming out of the nose and are indicated by a tilde, ~ .

a/ã	short sound like the 'u' in 'hut', except after 'p', 'b' and 'm' sounds, when it is more like the 'o' in 'not'		
	bas bus	*ãhã*	no
aa/aã	long sound, as the 'a' in 'garden'		
	aalu potato	*haãs*	duck
e/ẽ	as the 'é' in the French word 'soufflé'		
	peti belt	*garẽ*	I did
i/ī	always pronounced as the 'ee' in 'seem'		
	didi elder sister	*uhī*	he/she
o	as the 'o' in 'sold'		
	churot cigarette		
u/ū	as the 'oo' in 'boot'		
	lugaa clothes	*gaaū*	village
ai/aī	a diphthong, as the 'i' in 'mine'		
	salaai matches	*paītis*	thirty-five
au/aū	as the 'ow' in 'now' but shorter		
	mausam weather	*aūlo*	finger

7

Consonants

Most of the consonants are pronounced the same as in English. Most Nepali consonants can be doubled and must be pronounced with their full double force, as in Italian.

ch	as the 'ch' in 'chair' but with less breathiness
	charaa bird
j	as the 'j' in 'join' (some speakers pronounce it more like the 'dz' in 'adze')
	jaal net
n	as in English
	nilo blue
m	as in English
	aaimaai woman
y	as the 'i' in English 'view', but shorter
	syaau apple
r	always trilled slightly, and clearer than the English 'r'
	tarkaari vegetables
l	as in English but always clear
	asal good
w	as in English
	mwaai kiss
sh	as the 'sh' in 'short' (many speakers pronounce it as the English 's')
	desh country
s	as in English
	saano small
h	more forcefully than in English, except when it occurs in the middle of a word, in which case it is hardly pronounced at all
	hajaar thousand *ahile* now

ph   like 'ph' in 'haphazard' with a lot of breathiness,
        sometimes sounding like an 'f' made with both lips
           phal   fruit

Aspirated Consonants

These are an important part of Nepali pronunciation. They are pronounced much more forcefully than their unaspirated counterparts, with a lot of breath strongly exhaled, like the 'th' in 'hothouse'. English does have both types of consonant, but unlike Nepali, doesn't use them to differentiate between words. Aspiration is indicated by the letter 'h' following the consonant, so that 'th' represents an aspirated 't'. Don't confuse this with the English sound 'th', as in 'think' or 'then', which does not occur at all in Nepali.

Here are the consonants which occur both as aspirated and unaspirated sounds:

k	*kaataa*	fork	**kh**	*khaanaa*	food
g	*garmi*	hot	**gh**	*ghar*	house
ch	*chaamal*	rice	**chh**	*chhaataa*	umbrella
j	*juttaa*	shoe	**jh**	*jhyaal*	window
t	*tel*	oil	**th**	*thaal*	plate
d	*dahi*	yoghurt	**dh**	*dharma*	religion
p	*paani*	water	**ph**	*phul*	egg, flower
b	*bajaar*	market	**bh**	*bhoj*	feast

Retroflex Consonants

Retroflex sounds are made by curling your tongue up and back towards the roof of your mouth. In Nepali they occur with the 't' and 'd' sounds, ordinary and aspirated. They are not too difficult to get the hang of with a bit of practice. Try saying the sound several times, moving your tongue a bit further back along the

roof of your mouth each time. Retroflex consonants are indicated throughout the book with **bold** type.

t	*baato*	road	**th**	*kaathmaadaũ*	Kathmandu
d	*dũgaa*	boat	**dh**	*dhokaa*	door, gate

Word Stress
The position of the stressed syllable in Nepali words depends on the vowel length, and on whether the syllables are open, that is, they end in vowels, or closed, ending in consonants.

short vowels: a, ã, i, ĩ, u, ũ
long vowels: aa, aã, e, ẽ, ai, aĩ, o, au, aũ

In words of two syllables, if the last syllable is closed and contains a long vowel, then it is stressed. Otherwise the first syllable is stressed: (Stress is indicated here by an acute accent.)

cigarette	*chu-rót*
from now	*á-ba*

In words of more than two syllables, there are three possibilities:

1. If the second-to-last syllable is long, then it is stressed:

border	*si-maá-naa*

2. If the final syllable is closed with a long vowel or two consonants, then it is stressed:

India	*hin-du-staán*

3. If the second-to-last syllable is short and the last syllable is open, or closed with a short vowel and one consonant, then the third-to-last syllable is stressed:

lightweight   *há-lu-ko*

Grammar

This section contains some basic information about the structure of Nepali, and a few general grammar rules. It will enable you to learn the language quickly, to a point where you can communicate simply, by using different vocabulary items in the basic sentence patterns.

Word Order
The form of sentences in Nepali is different from English. The order in which words usually occur is subject-object-verb.

One of the distinguishing features of spoken Nepali is that it is often used in a kind of 'shorthand' way, when compared with written usage. Information that is clear from the context, or not relevant in a particular situation, will often be left out, such as subject pronouns.

Spoken Nepali is also sometimes grammatically simplified. For example, singular forms are often used with a plural meaning. Where such cases are very common, they have been indicated. However, it would be less colloquial, but not incorrect, to use only the strictly grammatical forms.

My name is Anita.   *mero naam anita ho*
This is my friend.   *yo mero saathi ho*

Nouns
Nouns in Nepali are single words, and there are no articles like English 'the' or 'a'. To make a noun plural, add the suffix *-haru*

12

to it, although this is often left out in speech when plurality is clear from context, or not relevant.

| a friend | *saathi* |
| friends | *saathiharu* |

Demonstratives

Because Nepali has no articles, the demonstratives 'this' and 'that' are in common use, both in front of nouns and alone.

| this | *yo* | these | *yi* |
| that | *tyo* | those | *ti* |

| this girl | *yo keti* | these girls | *yi ketiharu* |
| that girl | *tyo keti* | those girls | *ti ketiharu* |

Note that, in informal speech, the singular forms are often used even with plural subjects:

those people   *ti/tyo maanchheharu*

Adjectives

As in English, Nepali adjectives precede the noun they refer to:

an expensive shop   *mahāgo pasal*

To compare anything, use *-bhandaa*, 'than', or *sab-bhandaa*, 'than all':

Ram is fatter than Anita.	*ram anita-bhandaa moto chha*
Kathmandu is Nepal's largest city.	*kaathmaadaū nepaalko sab-bhandaa thulo shahar ho*

Pronouns

The Nepali pronominal system is a bit more complicated than the English system. Pronouns have both formal and informal variations, but you should normally use the formal forms, except with children and animals! Unless indicated otherwise, the formal (more polite) variation is used in this book.

Pronouns also have different case suffixes, that is, different endings according to their use in the sentence as a subject, object or possessive. These endings are translated as prepositions like 'to', 'of' and 'with' in English. However, as with nouns, there is no gender for pronouns, so that the English 'he', 'she' and 'it' share a single form in Nepali. Personal pronouns are often omitted in speech when they are clear from the context, as, for example, when they are the subject of the sentence.

Subject Pronouns (Nominative)

I	*ma*	we	*haami(haru)*
you (sg,inf)	*timi*	you (pl,inf)	*timiharu*
you (sg)	*tapaaī*	you (pl)	*tapaaīharu*

| he/she/it (inf) | *u, tyo, yo* | they (inf) | *uniharu* |
| he/she/it | *wahaā* | they | *wahaāharu* |

Note that for 'we', the short form *haami* is often used instead of the full form *haamiharu*; the brackets around *haru* indicate that it is optional. Note also that *u* and *uniharu* are used only for people, not things.

| I go | *ma jaanchhu* |
| he/she (inf) does | *u garchha* |

Subject Pronouns (Instrumental)

I	*maile*	we	*haami(haru)le*
you (sg,inf)	*timile*	you (pl,inf)	*timiharule*
you (sg)	*tapaaīle*	you (pl)	*tapaaīharule*
he/she/it (inf)	*usle, tyasle, yasle*	they (inf)	*uniharule*
he/she/it	*wahaāle*	they	*wahaāharule*

A transitive verb is one that takes an object. In Nepali, the subject of a transitive verb often appears in its instrumental form, that is, with *-le*. However this makes no difference to the meaning, and is just an idiomatic requirement of certain verbs and tenses. It translates as an ordinary subject in English: *maile bujhchhu*, I understand.

The instrumental case ending *-le* may also occur on nouns in certain idiomatic phrases, and may then be translated as 'by, with, from, of, in, etc', according to the context. Expressions of this kind must be learnt individually.

| 'in the opinion of the government' | *sarkaarko raayale* |

Object Pronouns (Accusative)

me	*malaai*	us	*haami(haru)laai*
you (sg,inf)	*timilaai*	you (pl,inf)	*timiharulaai*
you (sg)	*tapaaīlaai*	you (pl)	*tapaaīharulaai*
him/her/it (inf)	*uslaai, tyaslaai, yaslaai*	them (inf)	*uniharulaai*
him/her/it	*wahaālaai*	them	*wahaāharulaai*

In Nepali, the object of a transitive verb (whether direct or indirect) normally takes the accusative case ending *-laai*, particularly if the object is a name or refers to a person. In the following example, the ending *-laai* translates as 'to, for'.

I give it (to) you.   *ma timilaai dinchhu*

If a transitive object is nonhuman, *-laai* is usually left out.

He/She is feeding the dog.   *u kukur khuwaaūdaichha*

Possessive Pronouns

my	*mero*	our	*haamro*
your (sg,inf)	*timro*	your (pl,inf)	*timiharuko*
your (sg)	*tapaaīko*	your (pl)	*tapaaīharuko*
his/her/its (inf)	*usko, tyasko, yasko*	their (inf)	*uniharuko*
his/her/its	*wahaāko*	their	*wahaāharuko*

This is our dog.   *yo haamro kukur ho*

The possessive pronouns may also stand alone, in which case they translate as 'mine, ours, yours, his, hers, its, theirs'.

Is this yours?   *yo tapaaĩko ho?*

As in English, possessive adjectives precede the nouns they refer to.

Ram's shirt   *ramko kamij*

Verbs

There are very few irregular verbs in Nepali, so conjugation is fairly straightforward, except with the verb 'to be'. There are quite a few tenses, but it is really only necessary to learn the two present tenses, the past and future forms, and the imperative for orders and requests. As with pronouns, there are informal and formal forms for conjugating all these tenses, but again you'll find the formal style the most useful.

Nepali verbs are made up of two parts, the stem and the ending. Infinitives (the dictionary form) end in *-nu*:

to do	*garnu*
to eat	*khaanu*
to go	*jaanu*

Present – Simple Indefinite Tense

I do	*ma gar-chhu*
you (sg,inf) do	*timi gar-chhau*
he/she/it (inf) does	*u, tyo, yo gar-chha*
we do	*haami gar-chhaũ*
you (sg,inf) do	*timiharu gar-chhau*
they (inf) do	*uniharu gar-chha*

The formal forms all take the same ending:

you do	*tapaaī(haru) garnu-hunchha*
he/she/it does, they do	*wahaā(haru) garnu-hunchha*

Verbs whose stems end in a vowel keep the *n*, except when their stems end in *-aau* or *-iu*, in which case the *n* is not kept and the vowel is nasalised:

to go	*jaa-nu*
I go	*ma jaa-n-chhu*
to come	*aau-nu*
I come	*ma aaū-chhu*

The simple indefinite tense is used for regular or habitual actions, and corresponds to the simple present in English:

I work every day.	*ma dinhū kaam garchhu*

It can also be used to indicate the future:

Next year we are going to Nepal.	*aaune saal haami nepaal janchhaū*

Negation

There is no single form for negation in Nepali that corresponds to the English single form 'not'. All Nepali verb forms have separate negative forms, and must be learnt alongside the positive ones. Positive and negative forms are listed together in all verb sections.

You will see that some of the negatives have alternative forms.

In each case the first listed is the most common, and the other is a dialectal variant.

The simple indefinite negatives are listed here. The stem-final vowels of some verbs are nasalised, including the verb 'to go', *jaanu*.

I do not go	*ma jaā-dina/jaanna*
we do not go	*haami jaā-dainaū/jaannaū*
you (inf) do not go	*timi(haru) jaā-dainau/ jaannau*
he/she/it (inf) does not go	*u,tyo,yo jaā-daina/jaanna*
they (inf) do not go	*uniharu jaā-dainan/jaannan*

To negate formal forms, add *-hunna* to the infinitive:

you (sg) do not go	*tapaaī jaanu-hunna*
you (pl) do not go	*tapaaīharu jaanu-hunna*
he/she/it does not go	*wahaā jaanu-hunna*
they do not go	*wahaāharu jaanu-hunna*

Present Continuous Tense

This tense is formed with *-dai-* being inserted between the verb stem and the simple indefinite endings. In all verbs whose stems end in vowels, the vowel is also nasalised. The present continous is the most common tense in speech, and corresponds to the English present continous. Like the simple indefinite, it may also be used for future time.

I am eating	*ma khaā-dai-chhu*
you (sg) are eating	*timi khaā-dai-chhau*
he/she/it (inf) is eating	*u,tyo,yo khaā-dai-chha*
we are eating	*haami khaā-dai-chhaū*

you (pl) are eating	*timiharu khaā-dai-chhau*
they (inf) are eating	*uniharu khaā-dai-chhan*

Formal:

you (sg) are eating	*tapaaī khaā-dai-hunuhunchha*
you (pl) are eating	*tapaaīharu khaā-dai-hunuhunchha*
he/she/it is eating	*wahaā khaā-dai-hunuhunchha*
they are eating	*wahaāharu khaā-dai-hunuhunchha*

Past – Simple Past Tense

The simple past is used for completed past actions, and corresponds to the English simple past. The subject of a transitive verb (a verb that requires an object) in the simple past always takes the instrumental case ending *-le*:

I did/didn't	*maile garē/garinā*
you (sg,inf) did/didn't	*timile garyau/garenau*
he/she/it (inf) did/didn't	*usle, tyasle, yasle garyo/garena*
we did/didn't	*haamile garyaū/garenaū*
you (pl,inf) did/didn't	*timiharule garyau/garenau*
they (inf) did/didn't	*uniharule gare/garenan*

The formal terms add *-bhayo* and *-bhaena* to the infinitive:

you (sg) did/didn't	*tapaaīle garnu-bhayo/garnu-bhaena*
you (pl) did/didn't	*tapaaīharule garnu-bhayo/ garnu-bhaena*
he/she/it did/didn't	*wahaāle garnu-bhayo/garnu-bhaena*
they did/didn't	*wahaāharule garnu-bhayo/garnu-bhaena*

He/She/It (They) did not speak. *wahaã(harule) bolnu-bhaena*

In this tense, verbs with one-syllable stems ending in *-u*, change to *-o*:

to wash	*dhunu*
(I) wash	*dhun-chhu*
(I) washed	*dho-ē*

Verbs with vowel-final stems of two or more syllables drop the final vowel:

to forget	*birsanu*
(I) forget	*birsan-chhu*
(I) forgot	*birs-ē*

to come	*aaunu*
(I) come	*aau-chhu*
(I) came	*aa-ē*

Future

The most common future tense used in speech in Nepali is formed with a verb in the simple indefinite followed by the third person singular future form of 'to be', *hunu: holaa*.

I will go.	*ma jaanchhu holaa*
He/She will not go.	*u jaãdaina holaa*

The Neutral Tense

In conversation, Nepalese very commonly use a neutral verb form for present, and especially future, tenses. It is used mainly in short statements and questions, and pronouns are usually left out. The

ending *-ne* replaces the infinitive ending *-nu* to form this neutral tense; and its negative is formed simply with the prefix *na-*:

What will we do today?	*aaja ke garne?*
Let's go out.	*baahira jaane*
Let's not go out.	*baahira najaane*

'To Be'
The Nepali verb 'to be', *hunu*, has three alternate versions: *chha*, *ho* and *hunchha*.

Chha and *ho* both mean 'is' but *chha* is used for locating, that is, indicating where, and *ho* is used for defining, that is, indicating who, how, what.

Simple Present
chha
I am/am not	*ma chhu/chhaina*
you (sg,inf) are/are not	*timi chhau/chhainau*
he/she/it (inf) is/is not	*u, tyo, yo chha/chhaina*
we are/are not	*haami chhāu/chhaināu*
you (pl,inf) are/are not	*timiharu chhau/chhainau*
they (inf) are/are not	*uniharu chhan/chhainan*

ho
I am/am not	*ma hū/hoina*
you (sg,inf) are/are not	*timi hau/hoinau*
he/she/it (inf) is/is not	*u, tyo, yo ho/hoina*
we are/are not	*haami haū/hoinaū*
you (pl,inf) are/are not	*timiharu hau/hoinau*
they are/are not	*uniharu hun hoinan*

My house is in Nepal.   *mero ghar nepaalmaa chha*
My mother is a doctor.   *mero aamaa daaktar ho*

hunchha
Hunu also has a regular set of simple indefinite forms, from the
stem *hu-* and the usual simple indefinite endings. The negative
has alternative forms, the second indicated within brackets:

I am/am not   *ma hunchhu/hūdina (hunna)*
you (sg,inf) are/are not *timi hunchhau/hūdainau (hunnau)*
he/she/it is/is not   *u,tyo,yo hunchha/hūdaina (hunna)*
we are/are not   *haami hunchhaū/hūdainaū (hunnaū)*
you (pl,inf) are/are not *timiharu hunchhau/hūdainau (hunnau)*
they (inf) are/are not   *uniharu hunchhan/hūdainan (hunnan)*

The formal versions are the same for *chha*, *ho* and *hunchha*:

you (sg) are/are not   *tapaaī hunuhunchha/hunuhunna*
you (pl) are/are not   *tapaaīharu hunuhunchha/hunuhunna*
he/she/it is/is not   *wahaā hunuhunchha/hunuhunna*
they are/are not   *wahaāharu hunuhunchha/hunuhunna*

Hunchha also translates as 'is', but, unlike *chha* or *ho*, *hunchha*
refers to general facts or events:

This mango is sweet.   *yo aāp guliyo chha/ho*
Mangoes are sweet.   *aāp guliyo hunchha*

Simple Past
chha & ho
I was/was not   *ma thiē/thiinā*
you (sg,inf) were/were not *timi thiyau/thienau*

he/she/it (inf) was/was not	*u, tyo, yo thiyo/thiena*
we were/were not	*haami thiyaū/thienaū*
you (pl,inf) were/were not	*timiharu thiyau/thienau*
they were/were not	*uniharu thie/thienan*

The formal forms are as follows:

you (sg) were/were not	*tapaaī hunuhunthyo/hunuhunnathyo*
you (pl) were/were not	*tapaaīharu hunuhunthyo/hunuhunnathyo*
he/she/it was/was not	*wahāa hunuhunthyo/hunuhunnathyo*
they were/were not	*wahaāharu hunuhunthyo/hunuhunnathyo*

hunchha

I was/was not	*ma bhaē/bhainā*
you (sg,inf) were	*timi bhayau/bhaenau*
he/she/it was/was not	*u/tyo/yo bhayo/bhaena*
we were/were not	*haami bhayaū/bhaenaū*
you (pl,inf) were/were not	*timiharu bhayau/bhaenau*
they were/were not	*uniharu bhae/bhaenan*

The formal forms are as follows:

you (sg) were/were not	*tapaaī hunubhayo/hunubhaena*
you (pl) were/were not	*tapaaīharu hunubhayo/hunubhaena*
he/she/it was/was not	*wahāa hunubhayo/hunubhaena*
they were/were not	*wahaāharu hunubhayo/hunubhaena*

The verb *bhayo* is often pronounced just *bho*, especially when used as a common interjection meaning 'enough, stop'. It may also mean 'became' in a number of idioms:

| What's the matter? | *ke bhayo/bho?* |
| It has become hot. | *garmi bhayo* |

Hunchha and *hūdaina* may be translated as 'it is permissible' and 'it is forbidden' respectively, when used after another form of the infinitive, that which ends in *-na* instead of *-nu*. In this case the subject is usually omitted and, if expressed, takes *-le*:

| Is it alright to go there? | *tyahaā jaana hunchha?* |
| Children should not drink alcohol. | *ketaketile raksi khaana hūdaina* |

'To Have'

In Nepali there is no verb equivalent to the English 'to have', but the idea of possession may be expressed using a form of 'to be', *chha*, plus a possessive noun or pronoun:

| He/She has five children. | *usko paāchjanaa chhoraachhori chhan* |

If the possession is portable, the postpositions for 'with', *-sāga* and *-sita* are added to the possessor:

| I don't have a pen. | *masāga kalam chhaina* |

Imperative

This verb form is used for giving orders or making requests. There are informal and formal versions, but you need only learn the formal ones. To make an imperative, add the suffix *-hos* to the infinitive ending *-nu*. To make it negative, use the prefix *na-*:

| Please eat. | *khaanu-hos* |
| Please don't tell me. | *malaai na-bhannu-hos* |

Obligation

To express necessity, use the infinitive *-nu* plus a third person singular form of the verb *parnu*. The subject is usually omitted, and if expressed takes *-laai* with an intransitive verb and *-le* with a transitive verb:

It is necessary to walk there.	*tyahaā hīdnuparchha*
It isn't necessary to come to this office.	*yo kaaryaalayamaa aaunupardaina*
I have to wash these clothes.	*maile yo lugaa dhunuparchha*

Want & Need

The verb 'to be needed', *chaahinu*, is more common than 'to want', *chaahanu*. The simple past form *chaahiyo* is used for specific instances of want or need, such as 'it is needed now' or 'it was needed'. The simple indefinite *chaahinchha* is used to refer to want or need generally, and may be translated as 'it is generally needed' or 'it will be needed'. The subject takes the accusative case ending *-laai*:

| Do you want some tea? | *tapaaīlaai chiyaa chaahiyo?* |
| People need food. | *maanchheharulaai khaanaa chaahinchha* |

'To Be Able'

There are two ways of translating 'to be able' (or 'can') in Nepali. *Saknu* carries the idea of physical ability, while *paaunu* gives more a sense of favourable circumstances. Both are used with a *-na* infinitive:

I can (am able to) swim.   *ma paudi khelna sakchhu*
I can (manage to) get up early. *ma chãadai uthna paaũchhu*

In the past tense, the subject takes the instrumental ending *-le* if the infinitive takes an object:

I could not (wasn't able to)   *maile tyo pahaad chadhna*
   climb that hill.   *sakinã*

Questions

In Nepali the simplest way to ask a question is to raise the intonation of your voice at the end of the sentence. Answer this type of question by repeating the main verb in the affirmative or negative:

Are you Nepalese?   *tapaaĩ nepaali hunuhunchha?*
Yes.   *hunuhunchha*
No.   *hunuhunna*

You can also use interrogative words such as the following:

where	*kahaã*	what	*ke*
when	*kahile*	why	*kina*
how (means)	*kasari*	who	*ko*
whose	*kasko*	which	*kun*
how (quality)	*kasto*	someone	*kohi*
how much/ many	*kati*	something	*kehi*

Where is the tiger?   *baagh kahaã chha?*
Whose book is this?   *yo kitaab kasko ho?*

Prepositions

In Nepali prepositions follow the noun they refer to, and are usually called postpositions. They can also be used with adverbs and personal pronouns.

in front of	*-agaadi*	by, with	*-le*
out(side)	*-baahira*	at, in, on	*-maa*
from (place)	*-baata*	up	*-maathi*
in(side)	*-bhitra*	under	*-muni*
between	*-bich*	near, close	*-najik*
without	*-bina*	behind	*-pachhaadi*
from	*-dekhi*	after	*-pachhi*
of	*-ko*	with, by	*-sāga, sita*
for (the sake of)	*-kolaagi*	far	*-taadhaa*
to	*-laai*	about	*-tira*

Conjunctions

and	*ra*	but	*tara*
and then	*ani*	or	*ki*
because	*kinabhane*	otherwise	*natra*

'Other'

There are two words in Nepali meaning 'other': *arko*, 'the other of two' is used mainly with singular nouns, while *aru* 'other, else' is used with plural nouns and things that can't be counted:

I'll give you the other book.	*tapaaīlaai arko kitaab dinchhu*
Drink some more tea.	*aru chiyaa khaanuhos*

Greetings & Civilities

The Nepalese are very friendly people and love to chat, *gaph garnu* – you could call it a national pastime! So you won't find any barriers to conversation, which will probably proceed in a mixture of Nepali and English. English is compulsory for several years in Nepalese schools, and many people will be eager to practise it with you, especially in urban and popular tourist areas.

However, the use of even a few limited Nepali phrases will always increase your prospects for a mutually satisfying interaction. Attempting to communicate on a local level will add to your understanding and enjoyment of Nepal, and ensure your share of warm Nepalese hospitality is even warmer!

Greetings

The first thing you need to know is the general Nepali greeting, *namaste*. This expression covers all sorts of situations, from 'hello' to 'goodbye', for any time of the day, and the Nepalese consider it appropriate between all people. *Namaste* literally means 'I bow to the god in you' and is always a nice thing to say.

Namaskaar is an even more polite form of the same greeting, but less commonly used. Both should be accompanied by the gesture of palms held together in front of the face, as if in prayer.

Hello/Goodbye.	*namaste, namaskaar*
How are you?	*tapaaīlaai kasto chha?*
How are you? (formal)	*aaraamai hunuhunchha?*
I'm fine.	*malaai sanchai chha*

Please & Thank You

The Nepali word for 'please', *kripayaa*, is very formal and rarely used in speaking, being reserved mainly for writing. Instead, spoken Nepali uses the imperative verb suffix *-hos* (discussed in the Grammar chapter). Similarly, the word for 'thank you', *dhanyabaad*, is not used as commonly as the English word, since gratitude is expressed differently in Nepali than in English. It would be inappropriate to use *dhanyabaad* in shops or restaurants. Get used to the Nepalese social custom of not thanking, or use the English word where it is understood. *Dhanyabaad* is best kept to express thanks for particular favours.

Hajur

This is a handy word, which can be used in several different ways. It literally means 'sir', but there is no exact equivalent in English. *Hajur* may be used for both sexes. If someone calls you, *hajur?* is the correct response. It is also used to express agreement or confirm what someone has just said to you. *Hajur* may be added to the answer of a simple yes/no question, for the sake of politeness. But for the learner its greatest usefulness lies in the fact that if you did not hear or understand something said to you, and want it repeated, you need simply say *hajur?*

Attracting Someone's Attention

To attract someone's attention, call *o*, plus one of the kinship terms you'll find listed in the Small Talk chapter. Then say *namaste* and make your request. For the proprietor of a shop, restaurant, hotel or guesthouse, there is a special form of address.

Excuse me, sir.	*o, daai*
Excuse me, madam.	*o, didi*

| proprietor (male) | *saahuji* |
| proprietor (female) | *saahuni* |

Other Civilities

Other polite phrases used when meeting people, whether for the first time or not, include the following:

Where are you going?	*tapaaī kahaā jaanuhunchha?*
Where do you live/ Where are you staying?	*tapaaī kahaā basnuhunchha?*
Have you eaten?	*khaanaa khaanu bhayo?*
I hope we meet again!	*pheri bhetaūlaa!*

There is no special word for 'goodbye', but *namaste* can be used. Note that when addressing someone by name, the Nepalese usually add the suffix *-ji* (or sometimes *-jyu*, as in *daajyu* above) to the name as a sign of respect or affection.

| Ram, where are you going? | *ramji, tapaā kahaā jaanuhunchha?* |

Small Talk

Help!
Language Difficulties

Please write that down.	*malaai tyo kuraa lekh dinuhos*
I understand/understood.	*ma bujhchhu/maile bujhē*
I don't understand.	*maile bujhina*
Please say it again.	*pheri bhannuhos*
Please speak more slowly.	*bistaarai bolnuhos*
I will look for it in this book.	*yo kitaabmaa herdaichhu*
Please wait a minute.	*ek chhin parkhanuhos*
How do you say …?	*… laai ke bhannchha?*
I know/don't know.	*malaai thaahaa chha/chhaina*
Do you speak English?	*tapaaīāgreji bolna saknuhunchha?*
I only speak a little Nepali.	*ma ali ali nepaali bolchhu*
Do you speak (language name)?	*tapaaī (country name) ko bhaasaa bolnuhunchha?*
I speak (language name).	*ma (country name) bhaasaa bolchhu*

Top 10 Useful Phrases

Hello/Goodbye.	*namaste*
Yes. (definition)	*ho*
Yes. (location)	*chha*
No. (definition)	*hoina*
No. (location)	*chhaina*
Excuse me? (I didn't hear/understand)	*hajur?*

How much is it?	*kati ho?*
What is this/that?	*yo/tyo ke ho?*
Where are you going?	*tapaaaī kahaā jaanuhunchha?*
Is this the way to ...?	*... jaane baato yehi ho?*
What's the matter?	*ke bhayo?*
What's to be done?	*ke garne?*

It is very easy to strike up a conversation with the Nepalese, and you'll be asked all sorts of questions about how you like Nepal, where you come from, your family and so on.

Meeting People

My name is ...	*mero naam ... ho*
What is your name?	*tapaaīko naam ke ho?*
Where do you come from?	*tapaaīko ghar kahaā chha?*
Where do you live/are you staying?	*tapaaī kahaā basnuhunchha?*

Forms of Address

The Nepalese use kinship terms not only with their family but also with friends and even strangers, including foreigners. These terms are used far more commonly than names, so get used to calling people 'brother' and 'sister', and receiving the same in return! The term you use depends on whether the person is older or younger than you. Terms used for older people are generally more polite.

| father | *buwaa, baa* |
| mother | *aamaa* |

grandfather	*baaje*
grandmother	*bajyai*
elder brother	*daai, daajyu*
elder sister	*didi*
younger brother	*bhaai*
younger sister	*bahini*

Other Family Terms

brothers	*daajyubhaai*
children	*chhoraachhori*
daughter	*chhori*
family	*paribaar*
husband – own	*logne*
– someone else's	*srimaan*
sisters	*didibahini*
son	*chhoraa*
wife – own	*swaasni*
– someone else's	*srimati*

Are you married?	*tapaaĩko bihaa bhayo?*
I am married/single.	*mero bihaa bhayo/bhayo chhaina*
Is your husband/wife here?	*tapaaĩko srimaan/srimati yahaã chha?*
Do you have a boyfriend/ girlfriend?	*tapaaĩko prem/premi chha?*
Do you have any children?	*tapaaĩko chhoraachhori chhan?*
I don't have any children.	*chhoraachhori chhaina*
How many children?	*chhoraachhori kati janaa?*

I have two children.	*mero duijanaa chhoraachhori chhan*
I have a daughter/son.	*mero ekjanaa chhori/chhoraa cha*
Are your parents alive?	*aamaa, buwaa chhan?*
How many brothers do you have?	*kati janaa daajyubhaai chhan?*
How many sisters?	*kati janaa didibahini?*
How many in your family?	*tapaaīko paribaarmaa kati janaa chhan?*

Nationalities

I am from ...	*mero ghar ... ho*
Africa	*aphrikaa*
Australia	*astreliyaa*
Bangladesh	*bāglaadesh*
Belgium	*beljiyam*
Burma	*barmaa*
Canada	*kanadaa*
China	*chin*
Egypt	*misra*
England	*īglaīd*

France	*phraans*
Germany	*jarman*
Greece	*grunaan*
Holland	*halaīd*
India	*hindustaan, bhaarat*
Indonesia	*indonishyaa*
Iran	*iraan*
Ireland	*aairalaīd*
Israel	*ijraail*
Italy	*itali*
Japan	*jaapaan*
Malaysia	*maaleshiyaa*
Nepal	*nepaal*
New Zealand	*nyujilaīd*
Pakistan	*paakistaan*
Russia	*rus*
Spain	*spen*
Sri Lanka	*srilākaa*
Taiwan	*chin janabaadi ganatātra*
Thailand	*thaailaīd*
Tibet	*tibbat, bhot*
Turkey	*tarki*
USA	*amerikaa*
Vietnam	*bhiyatnaam*

Age

How old are you?	*tapaaī kati barsa bhayo?*
	tapaaīko umer kati ho?
I am … years old	*ma … barsa bhayo*
18	*athaara*
25	*pachchis*

Occupations

What is your occupation?	*tapaaī ke kaam garnuhunchha?*
Where do you work?	*tapaaī kahaā kaam gar-nuhunchha?*

I am a/an ...	*ma ... hū*
actor/artist	*kalaakaar*
architect	*silpakar*
businessperson	*bepaari*
clerk	*kaarindaa*
dancer	*naachne maanchhe*
doctor	*daaktar*
engineer	*injiniyar*
factory worker	*kaarkhaanaako majdur*
farmer	*kisaan*
journalist	*patrakaar*
lawyer	*wakil*
musician	*sāgitkaar*
nurse	*parichaarikaa*
office worker	*karmachaari*
police officer	*pulis*
priest	*pujaari*
scientist	*baigyaanik*
secretary	*sachib*
soldier	*sipaahi*
student	*bidyaarthi*
tailor	*suchikaar*
teacher	*sichek*
traveller	*yaatri*
waiter	*beraa*
writer	*lekhak*

Religion

What is your religion?	*tapaaīkun dharma maanuhunchha?*
Buddhism	*buddha dharma*
Christianity	*isaai dharma*
Hinduism	*hindu dharma*

I am Jewish.	*ma yahudi hū*
I am a Muslim.	*ma musalmaan hū*
I am not religious.	*ma kunai dharma maandinā*

Yes & No

There are various ways of answering 'yes' or 'no' to questions. If using body language, nodding means 'yes' and a sideways shake of the head means 'no', as in English. However, there is a kind of sideways tilt of the head, accompanied by a slight shrug of the shoulders, that the Nepalese often use to indicate agreement, during bargaining, for instance. Don't mistake this for a 'no'. Yes/no questions are also commonly answered by repeating the main verb in the affirmative or negative. This will often involve some form of the verb 'to be'; *chha, ho* or *hunchha*.

yes	*ã*
yes (agreement)	*hajur*
yes (definition)	*ho*
OK (very polite)	*haas*
yes (location)	*chha*
OK, I see.	*achchhaa*
yes (permitted), OK (polite)	*hunchha*
oh	*aoho, e, i*

no	*ahā*
no (not able)	*sakdaina*
no (definition)	*hoina*
no (not available)	*paaindaina*
no (location)	*chhaina*
no (not permitted)	*hūdaina*

Feelings

I am/am not ...	*malaai ... laagyo/laagena*
angry	*ris*
annoyed	*dikka*
cold	*jaado*
drunk	*raksi*
happy	*khusi*
hot	*garmi*
hungry	*bhok*
in a hurry	*hataar*
lost	*haraauna*
right	*thik*
sad, sorry	*dukha*
scared	*dar*
sick	*biraami*
sleepy	*nidraa*
thirsty	*tirkhaa*
tired	*thakaai*
windblown	*haawaa*
worried	*pir*
wrong	*bethik*

Some Useful Phrases

How do you like Nepal?	*tapaaĩlaaĩ nepaal kasto laagyo?*
I like it a lot.	*malaai ekdam raamro laagyo*
What do you do in your free time?	*chhuttiko samaymaa ke gar nuhunchha?*
Do you like …?	*tapaaĩlaaĩ … manparchha?*
I like/don't like …	*malaai … man parchha/pardaina*
dancing	*naachna*
films	*sinemaa, philam herna*
shopping	*kinmel garna*
music	*sāgit sunna*
playing games	*khel garna*
playing/watching sport	*khelkud khelna/herna*
reading	*padhna*
travelling	*yaatraa garna*
watching TV	*telibhijan herna*
playing cards	*tash khelna*
It's fun (to do).	*(garna) majaa laagchha*

Getting Around

Finding Your Way

The Nepalese are helpful in giving directions, and may even offer to escort you to your destination. It isn't difficult to get lost as you walk along winding alleys and trails, but it's the best way to see interesting local scenes. Nepali has a small vocabulary compared with English, so English words are used for many modern things.

How do I get to …?	… *kasaari jaane?*
Could you tell me where … is?	… *kahaā chha?*
Is this the way to …?	*yo baato … jaane ho?*
Is it far from here?	*yahaābaata taadhaa chha?*
Can I walk there?	*hĩdera jaana sakinchhu?*
Is it difficult to get there?	*jaana gaahro chha?*
What … is this?	*yo kun … ho?*
road	*baato*
place	*thaaũ*

Directions — Dishaa

across	*paari*
along	*bhari*
back, behind	*pachhaadi*
beside	*chheumaa*
down, below	*tala*
in front of	*agaadi*
inside, into	*bhitra*

left	*bayaā*
middle, centre	*bich*
on	*maa*
out, outside	*baahira*
over, above	*maathi*
over there	*u tyahaā*
right	*daayaā*
side	*patti, chheu*
towards	*tira*
up there	*u maathi*

Getting Around

There are all sorts of ways of travelling around Nepal. There are no trains, and much of the country can only be reached by walking or flying. In towns, rickshaws, autorickshaws and taxis are commonly available and inexpensive. It is customary to bargain over the cost for a particular journey, even with taxi drivers, who often refuse to use their meters. They are also notorious for being unable to change large bills and not carrying any small change, so try to keep some with you. Town buses are very cheap but always extremely crowded and slow. Country buses, especially tourist ones, aren't so bad. Taxis and chauffeur-driven cars are readily available for longer trips, but are expensive, as are motorbikes for hire. Bicycles are the cheapest form of urban transport and often the most convenient, as taxis after dark are difficult to find and charge twice, or even more, the meter fare.

Is a/an … available here?	*yahaa … paainchha?*
autorickshaw	*tyaampu*
bicycle	*saikal*
bus	*bas*

car	*motar*
rickshaw	*rikshaa*
taxi	*tyaaksi*
vehicle	*gaadi*

Buying Tickets

I want to go to …	*ma … jaanchhu*
How much is it to go to …?	*… kolaagi kati paisaa laagchha?*
How can I get to …?	*… kasaari jaane?*
Is there a flight to …?	*… maa plen jaanchha?*
Is there another way to get there?	*arko kasaari jaane?*
I want a one-way/return ticket.	*jaane/jaane-aaune tikat dinuhos*
How long does the trip take?	*pugnalaai kati samay laagchha?*
How much is a bicycle per hour/day?	*saikal ghantaako/dinko kati ho?*

What time does it …?	*kati baje …?*
arrive	*auune, pugne*
leave	*jaane*
return	*pharkane*

Bus

Does this bus go to …?	*yo … jaane bas ho?*
Where does this bus go?	*yo bas kahaā jaane?*
Is the bus completely full?	*bas paryo?*
Are there any stops?	*katai rokchha?*
Will it be on time?	*samaymaa pugchha?*
Is that seat taken?	*yahaā kohi maanchhe chha?*

Please tell me when we get to ...

... aae pachhi bas rokidinuhos

I want to get off here.

ma yahaã orlinchhu

When is the ... trip?
next
first
last

... yaatraa kahile jaane?
arko
pahila
antim

Taxi/Autorickshaw

Can you take me to ...?	*... maaj laanuhunchha?*
For two people?	*duijanaako laagi?*
Does that include the luggage?	*saamaansamet garera?*
How much do I owe you?	*kati paisaa dinuparchha?*
Is it far from here?	*yahaābaata ke taadhaa chha?*
It is near here.	*najik chha*

Instructions

Go straight ahead.	*sidhaa jaanuhos*
Turn left/right.	*bayaā/dayaā modnuhos*
Drive slowly.	*bistaarai haāknuhos*
Please hurry.	*chito garnuhos*
Be careful!	*hos garnuhos!*
Stop!	*roknuhos!*
Keep going.	*jaādai garnuhos*

Some Useful Words

address	*thegaanaa*
boat	*dūgaa*
to cancel	*radda garnu*
to confirm	*pakkaa garnu*
corner	*kunaa*
customs	*bhansaar*
early	*saberai*
fast	*chito*
late	*dhilo, aberai*
map	*naksaa*
plane	*hawaaijahaaj, plen*
to be seated	*basi raakhnu*

to stand	*ubhinu*
to be standing	*uthi raakhnu*
ticket	**tikat**
timetable	*samaya taalikaa*
to travel	*yaatraa garnu*
to tour, walk	*ghumnu*
to wait	*parkhanu*
to walk	*hī**d**nu*

Accommodation

In Kathmandu all types of accommodation are available, ranging from international-standard five-star hotels, to small guesthouses with picturesque roof gardens, and tiny lodges with very basic facilities and rock-bottom prices. There is a 10% to 15% government tax added to the bill, and occasionally an extra service charge.

Outside Kathmandu accommodation varies considerably. In towns and tourist centres such as the Chitwan National Park, both the range and prices are similar to those in the capital. In the country most hotels and lodges are modestly priced, but standards differ so it is worth checking a few places in the same location.

Accommodation on trekking routes may be particularly primitive, especially in remote areas. More popular trekking routes are becoming lined with lodges offering, but not necessarily being able to provide, all kinds of facilities from hot water to Western-style food. Again, comparing a few establishments is worthwhile. If you arrange for an evening meal on less popular trekking routes, the price quoted to you traditionally includes accommodation for the night, but do ask.

If you are staying in one area for some time, most guesthouses don't mind some food preparation in your room. So try to get a place near a local market, as fridges are a luxury item in Nepal and rarely provided even in expensive accommodation.

Finding Accommodation

Where is a ...? ... *kahaā chha?*
  guesthouse *paunaghar*

hotel	*hotel*
lodge	*laaj*

What is the address?	*thegaanaa ke ho?*
Please write down the address.	*thegaanaa lekhnuhos*

I am looking for a ...	*ma ... khojeko*
cheap lodge	*sasto laaj*
good hotel	*raamro hotel*
nearby hotel	*najik hotel*
clean hotel	*saphaa hotel*

At the Hotel
Checking In

Do you have any rooms?	*kothaa paainchha?*
I would like a ...	*ma ... chaahinchha*
single room	*ekjanaakolaagi kothaa*
double room	*duijanaakolaagi kothaa*

I want a room with ...	*malaai ... bhaeko kothaa chaahinchha*
hot water	*tato paani*
a window	*jhyaal*

How much is it per night?	*ek raatko, kati paisaa ho?*
Does it include breakfast?	*bihaanako khaanaa samet ho?*
Can I see the room?	*kothaa herna sakinchha?*
Are there any others?	*arko kothaa paainchha?*
Are there any cheaper rooms?	*arko kunai sasto kothaa chha?*

Do you allow children?	*bachchaapani basnuhunchha ki hūdaina?*
Is there a discount for children?	*ke bachchaakolaagi kam hunchha?*
Does the hotel have a restaurant?	*hotelmaa bhojanaalaya chha?*

Some Useful Phrases

Is ... available?	*... paainchha?*
a garden	*bagaĩchaa*
food	*khaanaa*
tea, coffee	*chiyaa, kaphi*
boiled water	*umaaleko paani*

The room is ...	*kothaa ... chha*
big	*thulo*
small	*saano*
clean	*saphaa*
dirty	*phohor*
cheap	*sasto*
expensive	*mahãgo*

Please give me ...	*malaai ... dinuhos*
bedding	*bichhaaunaa*
breakfast	*bihaanako khaanaa*
a candle	*mainbatti*
a chair	*mech*
a curtain	*pardaa*
a fan	*pākhaa*

I'm staying for ...	*ma ... baschhu*
one night	*ek raat*
three nights	*tin raat*
a week	*ek haptaa*

I'm not sure how long I'll stay. — *kati basne malaai thaahaa chhaina*

Where is the toilet?	*charpi kahaã chha?*
Is there hot water all day?	*dinbhari tato paani aaũchha?*
Is there somewhere to wash clothes?	*lugaa dhune thaaũ paainchha?*
Do I leave my key at reception?	*saãcho risaapchanmaa chodne?*
Do you have a safe?	*tapaaĩkahaã surakshit thaaũ chha?*

Could you store this for me?	*yo chodna sakinchha?*
Could I use the telephone?	*ma phon garna sakchhu?*
Could someone look after my child?	*mero bachchaalaai herna sakinchha?*
Please wake me up at ... o'clock tomorrow morning.	*malaai bholi bihaana ... baje uthaunuhos*
Please clean the room.	*kothaa saphaa garnuhos*
Please change the sheets.	*tannaa phernuhos*

first name	*subhanaam*
surname	*thar*
room number	*kothaako nambar*

Requests & Complaints

Excuse me, there's a problem with my room.	*o saahuji, mero kothaamaa samasyaa bhayo*
I have a request.	*euta anurodh chha*
The window doesn't open/close.	*jhyaal kholna/launa sakena*
I've locked myself out.	*saãcho kothaamaa paryo*
The toilet won't flush.	*charpi kam gardaina*
There's no (hot) water.	*(tato) paani chhaina*
The ... doesn't work.	*... kam gardaina*
Can you get it fixed?	*yo banaauna sakchha?*
I don't like this room.	*malaai yo kothaa manpardaina*

It's too ...	*dherai ... chha*
small	*saano*
cold/hot	*chiso/tato*
dark	*ãdhyaaro*
noisy	*hallaa*
expensive	*mahãgo*

This room smells.	*yo kothaa ganaaũhha*

Checking Out

I would like to check out ...	*ma ... jaanchhu*
now	*ahile*
at noon	*baarha baje*
tomorrow	*bholi*

Can I leave my bags here?	*ke ma yahaã jholaa chodna sakinchha?*
I'd like to pay now.	*ma ahile paisaa tirchhu*

I'm coming back ...	*ma ... pharkinchhu*
in a few days	*ke din pachhi*
in two weeks	*dui haptaa pachhi*

Some Useful Words

address	*thegaanaa*
apartment	*deraa*
babysitter	*bachchaa herne maanchhe*
balcony	*baardali*
to bathe/shower	*nuhaaunu*
bed	*khaat*
blanket	*kambal*
candle	*mainbatti*
chair	*mech*
cheap	*sasto*
(to) clean	*saphaa (garnu)*
cold	*chiso* (touch), *jaado* (weather)
to cook	*pakaaunu*
cupboard	*daraaj*
dark	*āhyaaro*
dirty	*phohor*
to eat	*khaanu*
electricity	*bijuli*
excluded	*baahek*
expensive	*mahāgo*
fan	*pākhaa*
hot	*tato* (touch), *garmi* (weather)
hut	*chhaapro, jhupro*
including	*samet*
key	*saācho*
lightbulb	*chim*

lock	*chukul*
to lock	*taalchaa garnu*
mattress	**d**asanaa
mirror	*ainaa*
nanny	*dhaai*
pillow	*siraani*
quiet	*shaanta*
quilt	*sirak, o***d***hne
room	*kothaa*
sheet	*tannaa*
shelter	*baas*
to sleep	*sutnu*
soap	*saabun*
to stay	*basnu*
toilet	*charpi*
towel	*rumaal*
water	*paani*
window	*jhyaal*

Around Town

I'm looking for …	*ma … khojiraeko*
a bank	*baĩk*
my hotel	*mero hotel*
a market	*bajaar*
the museum	*samgrahaalaya*
the police	*prahari*
the post office	*hulaak addaa*
the … embassy	*… raajdutaavaas*
the tourist office	*paryatan kaaryaalaya*

What time does it open/ close?	*kati baje kholchha/banda garchha?*

At the Embassy

Where can I extend my visa?	*bhija kahaã thapnu?*
I want to extend my visa for … days.	*malaai … dinko laagi arko bhija dinuhos*
When can I collect my passport?	*mero raahadaani kahile lina aaunaa?*

At the Post Office

Nepal's postal service is not bad, but never post anything in letterboxes or give it to your hotel, and make sure you see the postal clerk cancel the stamps on your mail. There are very few post offices in Nepal and their hours are short, so there are usually queues.

I want to send ...   ... *pathaaunu manlaagchha*
  a letter   *chitthi*
  a parcel   *pulindaa*

Please give me some stamps.   *malaai tikat dinuhos*

How much is it to send ...?   *... ko laagi tikat kati laagchha?*
  an aerogram   *hawaaipatra*
  airmail   *hawaaidaak*

Telephone

I want to call ...   *malaai ... phon garnuparyo*
The number is ...   *nambar ... ho*
I want to speak for three   *tin minat phon garchhu*
minutes.
How much is it per minute?   *minatko kati ho?*
Hello, do you speak English?   *hello, āgreji bolnuhunchha?*
Is ... there?   *... chha?*
Yes, he/she is here.   *chha*
One moment.   *ek chhin*

At the Bank

Changing money in Nepalese banks is usually straightforward.
Unlike some other countries, hotel exchange counters and other
places that accept foreign currency don't normally charge more
than the bank rate. Be sure to keep all your exchange receipts if
you want to extend your visa or exchange rupees at the airport
when you leave.

I want to change some   *paisaa saatnu manlaagchha*
money.

What is the exchange rate today?	*aaja saatne ret kati chha?*
How many rupees per dollar?	*ek dollarko kati ho?*
Can I have money sent here from my bank?	*mero baīkbaata paisaa yahaā aaūchha?*
How long will it take?	*pugna kati samay laagchha?*
I'm expecting some money from …	*… baata paisaa apekshaa garchhu*
Has my money arrived yet?	*mero paisaa aayo?*
Can I change this note for smaller change?	*yallaai khudraa paisaa dinuhos*

Sightseeing

Nepal is full of fascinating historical and religious sights, and in many places local people will be happy to show you around and give background information. Most Nepalese love being photographed, but be sensitive and always ask first. There is very little nightlife in Kathmandu or other places, as most pubs and restaurants have to close at 10 pm. People tend to stay home after dark, but the streets are pretty safe at night.

Where is the tourist office?	*paryatan kaaryaalaya kahaā chha?*
What's that …?	*tyo … ke ho?*
building	*bhawan*
monument	*smaarak*
temple	*mandir*
How old is it?	*kati puraano bhayo?*
Who built it?	*kosle banaaeko?*
Can I take photos?	*tasbir khichnu hunchha?*

Can I take your photo?	*tapaaīko tasbir khichnu hunchha?*
I will send you the photo.	*tasbir tapaaīlaai pathaaunchhu*
Please write down your address.	*tapaaīko thegaanaa lekhnuhos*
Could you take my photo?	*mero tasbir khichnuhos*

Some Useful Words

ancient	*praachin*
cremation	*daahasāskaar*
cultural show	*saāskritik pradarshan*
dome	*stupaa*
gardens	*bagaīchaa*
ghat	*ghaat*
god/goddess	*deutaa*
monastery	*gumbaa*
mosque	*masjid*
old city	*puraano shahar*
pagoda	*gaajur*
palace	*darbaar*
religion	*dharma*
restaurant	*bhojanaalaya*
zoo	*chidiyaakhaanaa*

Trekking

Eight of the world's 14 highest mountains are found in Nepal, and its northern frontier is bordered by the mighty Himalaya, so Nepal is well known for having some of the best trekking in the world. Naturally most trekking areas are remote, and the Nepalese who live in the mountains and high valleys are more traditional than those in Kathmandu and other towns. They are devout and more observant of local customs, which are deeply rooted in their religion, a harmonious mixture of Hinduism and Buddhism. As you walk along you will come across holy buildings, stupas (white domes with prayer flags) and walls of prayer stones. Always keep these on your right as you pass.

Along the trails, and in villages, you will come across a kind of community resting place or meeting place, made by building rocks and stones into a comfortable seating area at the base of a shady tree - often a very large tree. This is called a *chautara* and the locals will be more than happy for you to join them there. *Chautaras* are easy to recognise and are commonly referred to when giving directions. They are also to be found in towns, and the most well-known is the one in New Rd, Kathmandu, where all the newspaper sellers, shoeshiners and camera shops are.

Nepali is not necessarily the main language spoken by the people you meet while trekking, but most will speak it well. The first person you could practise your new-found skills on is your porter, *bhariyaa*. Unless you choose relatively remote and less populous trekking routes, you'll have few difficulties with language, porters, equipment, accommodation or food. Foodstuffs can be scarce so be prepared to take whatever you find. Villagers will often offer to let you share their meal and home, but never

enter a house uninvited. Remember that the fireplace is sacred, so don't throw rubbish into it.

All villages have a communal toilet, *charpi*, which trekkers are welcome to use, and this is preferable to sullying the countryside. If you do toilet outside, keep well away from water sources, and out of sight. Dig a hole, and do burn your toilet paper, as nothing looks worse than piles of pink paper littering the landscape! The Nepalese don't use toilet paper and think it's pretty strange; besides, they don't have any. They use a waterjug, *lotaa*, and their left hand, which is naturally not used for anything else such as giving or receiving, or shaking hands!

Hiring Porters

Excuse me, brother, will you go with me?	*e, daajyu, tapaaī masāga jaane?*
Where do you want me to go?	*kahaā jaane ho?*
To Jomsom.	*jomsomsamma*
How long will it take, there and back?	*jaana, aauna, kati din laagchha?*
About 20 days.	*bis dinjati laagchha*
How much will you pay?	*paisaa kati dinuhunchha?*
How much are you asking?	*tapaaī kati bhannuhunchha?*
Without food?	*khaanaa nakhaera?*
With/Without a load?	*bhaari chha/chhaina?*
I'll give ... rupees per day.	*dinko ... rupaiyaā dinchhu*
OK. When do we go?	*hunchha. kahile jaane?*
At 6 o'clock tomorrow morning.	*bholi bihaana chha baje*
We'll meet at this hotel.	*yo hotelmaa bhetne*

Asking Directions

To get your bearings along the way, you'll probably need to ask directions, the names of villages and distances. When asking how long it takes to reach a destination, remember that locals travel faster than you! Distance is often measured in *kos*: one kos is about three km. If the answer is *dui kos*, two kos, this is not literally true but a common expression meaning 'not too far'.

Which is the way to Lukla?	*luklajaane baato kun ho?*
What is the next village?	*aaune gaaŭko naam ke ho?*
Is this the way to …?	*… jaane baato yehi ho?*
How far is it to …?	*… maa kati taadhaa parchha?*
How many hours/days?	*kati ghantaa/din?*
Which direction?	*kun dishaa?*
Where have you come from?	*kahaãbaata aaunubhaeko?*
From Pokhara.	*pokharaabaata*
It takes us three hours.	*haamilaai tin ghantaa laagchha*
For you it will take four to five hours.	*tapaaĩlaai chaar-paãch ghantaa laagchha*

north	*uttar*
south	*dakshin*
east	*purba*
west	*pashchim*
left	*bayaã*
right	*dayaã*
this side	*waari*
that side	*paari*
level	*samma*
upward	*maastira*

uphill	*ukaalo*
steep uphill	***thado***
downward	*talatira*
downhill	*oraalo*
steep downhill	*bhiraalo, paharilo*
straight ahead	*sidhaa*
a little	*ali ali*

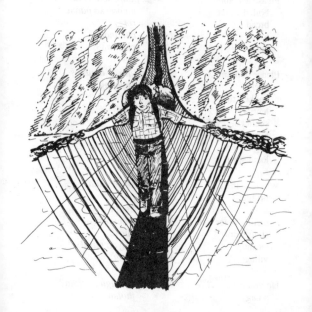

Along the Way

Where can I spend the night?	*baas basna kahaã paainchha?*
There are three of us.	*haami tin janaa chhaũ*
Do you provide meals?	*khaanaa paainchha ki?*
What kind of food?	*ke khaanaa paainchha?*

Please ask about ...	*... baare sodhnuhos*
boiled water	*umaaleko paani*
bread	*roti*
food	*khaanaa*
tea	*chiyaa*

Please give me ...	*malaai ... dinuhos*
beer	*chyaang*
cooked rice	*bhaat*
lentils	*daal*
shelter	*baas*
tobacco	*surti*
vegetables	*tarkaari*
local spirit	*rakshi*

Where is the ...?	*... kahaã chha?*
bridge	*pul*
inn	*bhatti*
resting place tree	*chautara*
statue/idol	*murti*
teashop	*chiyaa pasal*
village	*gaaũ*

Do you have ...?	*tapaaĩsāga ... chha?*
a bag	*jholaa*

a carrybasket	*doko*
firewood	*daauraa*
a knife	*chakku*
a large Nepalese knife	*khukuri*

What time are you ...?	*kati baje ...?*
getting up	*uthne*
going to sleep	*sutna jaane*

Some Useful Words

agriculture	*khetipaati*
bridge	*pul*
cave	*guphaa*
creek	*kholaa*
earthquake	*bhuĩchaalo*
farm	*khetbaari*
forest, jungle	*ban*
hanging bridge	*jhulunge pul*
hill	*pahaad*
hillperson	*pahaadi*
lake	*taal*
landslide	*pairo*
mountain	*himaal*
nature	*prakriti*
pass	*bhanjyaang*
peak	*chuchuro*
plains	*mades, taraai*
plainsdweller	*madesi*
pond	*pokhari*
river	*nadi*
scenery	*drishya*

trail	*saano baato*
waterfall	*jharnaa*

Weather
What's the weather like?

Mausam
mausam kasto chha?

The weather is ... today.	*aaja mausam ... chha*
Will it be ... tomorrow?	*bholi mausam ... holaa?*
bad/good	*kharaab/raamro*
cloudy/foggy	*badli/kuiro*
cold/hot	*jaado/garmi*
humid	*baaspiya*
lightning	*bijulichamkaai*
frost/snow	*tusaaro/hiũ*
rainy/sunny	*paani parchha/ghamailo*
thunder	*garjan*
windy	*haawaadaari*

Some Useful Words

summer	*garmi mausam*
autumn	*sharadritu*
winter	*jaado mahinaa*
spring	*basanta ritu*
blizzard	*hiũko aãdhi*
cloud	*baadal*
earth	*prithvi*
ice	*baraph*
monsoon	*barsaayukta*
mud	*hilo*
rainy season	*barsaayaam*

| soil | *maato* |
| thunderstorm | *meghgarjan tathaa barsaa* |

Animals   *Janaawarharu*

bear	*bhaalu*
buffalo (f)	*bhaĩsi*
buffalo (m)	*raãga*
cat	*biraalo*
cow	*gaai*
crocodile	*gohi*
deer	*mrigai*
dog	*kukur*
donkey	*gadhaa*
elephant	*hatti*
fish	*maachhaa*
fox	*phyaauro*
frog	*bhyaaguto*
goat	*bokaa, khasi*
horse	*ghodaa*
jackal	*syaal*
leopard	*chituwaa*
lion	*sĩha*
lizard	*chhepaaro*
mole	*chhuchundro*
mongoose	*nyaauri musaa*
monkey	*baãdar*
mouse, rat	*musaa*
ox	*goru*
pet	*paaltu janaawar*
pig	*sũgur*
rabbit	*kharaayo*

rhinoceros	*gaīdaa*
sheep	*bhedo*
snake	*saāp*
squirrel	*lokharke*
tiger	*baagh*
yak	*chaūrigaai*
yeti	*yeti*

Birds — *Charaaharu*

chicken	*kukhuraa*
crow	*kaag*
duck	*haās*
eagle, kite	*chil*
falcon	*baaj*
hen	*kukhuri*
owl	*ullu*

parrot	*sugaa*
peacock	*mayur*
pheasant	*kaalij*
pigeon	*parewaa*
rooster	*bhaale*
vulture	*giddha*

Insects   *Kiraaharu*

ant	*kamilaa*
bee	*mauri*
butterfly	*putali*
cockroach	*saāglo*
flea	*upiyaā*
fly	*jhīngaa*
leech, worm	*jukaa*
louse	*jumra*
mosquito	*laamkhutte*
spider	*maakuraa*
tick	*kirno*

Plants   *Biruwaaharu*

branch	*haāgaa*
bush	*jhaadi*
flower	*phul*
leaf	*paat*
rhododendron	*laali guraās*
stick	*latthi*
sugar cane	*ukhu*
tree	*rukh*
wood	*kaath*

Some Useful Phrases

Am I allowed to camp here?	*yahaã shibir garna hunchha?*
Is there a campsite nearby?	*ke tyahaã shibir najik chha?*
I want to hire (a) ...	*malaai ... bhaadaamaa*
	chaahiyo
backpack	*jholaa*
sleeping bag	*sutne jholaa*
stove	*chulo*
tent	*paal*
Can I get there on foot?	*tyahaã hĩdera jaana sakchha?*
Do I need a guide?	*baato dekhaaunu parchha?*
Can I swim here?	*yahaã paudi khelna sakchhu?*
What's that animal/plant called?	*tyo janaawar/biruwaa laai ke bhannchha?*
I want to look at your trekking permit.	*tapaaĩko anumatipatra hernuparchha*
Are you going by yourself?	*tapaaĩ eklaai jaane?*
I have to rest.	*malaai aaraam linuparchha*
Let's sit in the shade.	*shitalmaa basaũ*
Carry me slowly.	*malaai bistaarai boknuhos*
I have to urinate/defecate.	*malaai pisaab/dishaa laagyo*

Some Useful Words

to ask	*sodhnu*
to ask for	*maagnu*
big	*thulo*
cheap	*sasto*
to climb	*chadhnu*
to come	*aaunu*

difficult	*gaahro*
distance (3 km)	*kos*
down	*tala*
easy	*sajilo*
expensive	*mahãgo*
far	***taadhaa***
fast	*chito, chaãdai*
heavy	*gahraũ*
kerosene	***mattitel***
lamp, light	*batti*
mountaineer	*parbataarohi*
near	*najik*
now	*ahile*
OK	***thikchha***
shelter	*baas*
to sleep	*sutnu*
slow, late	***dhilo***
small	*saano*
stone	***dhungaa***
to trek	*paidal yaatraa garnu*
up	*maathi*
½ litre	*maanaa*
walk	*hĩdnu*

Food

In the restaurants of Kathmandu and other large towns, all kinds of dishes are available, including a wide range of Western-style food. But in the country, and on trekking routes, food is much simpler and at any one time of the year only a few different food items are available.

The most typical Nepali meal is *daal bhaat tarkaari*: boiled rice with lentils and vegetable curry. It is usually served with a fresh pickle or relish which may be very spicy, *piro*. However, in the hills, potatoes, corn, millet and other carbohydrates are also staple foods. Meat is scarce and expensive, and tends to be served mainly on festival days and other special occasions. Remember that in Hindu Nepal cows are sacred and beef is not eaten. The meat likely to be available is buff (water buffalo), *raãgako maasu*, goat, *khasiko maasu*, chicken, *kukhuraako maasu*, or yak, *chaũrigaaiko maasu*. If you don't want spicy food, request *piro nahaalnuhos*. Vegetarian meals are widely available due to both the fact that high-caste Hindus are traditionally vegetarians, and the scarcity of meat. In Nepal two meals a day are the norm, one around 10 or 11 am and the second at 7 or 8 pm, with just a glass of tea after getting up. In less touristy areas, you may not be able to get a Western-style breakfast, or any other type of food, before 10 am. The Nepalese usually eat with their hands – remember to use your right hand only and wash before and after eating.

breakfast	*bihaanako khaanaa*
lunch	*chamenaa*
dinner	*bhaat*
restaurant	*bhojanaalaya*

70

snack	*khaajaa*
teashop	*chiyaa pasal*
food, meal	*bhaat*
to drink	*piunu*
to eat	*khaanu*

The verb *khaanu* is also commonly used for drinking and smoking:

I eat rice.	*ma bhaat khaanchhu*
I drink tea.	*ma chiyaa khaanchhu*
I smoke cigarettes.	*ma churot khaanchhu*

At the Restaurant

Waiter!	*daajyu!* (man)/*bhaai!* (boy)
	didi! (woman)/*bahini!* (girl)
Please show me the menu.	*menu dinuhos*

Can I have a little ...?	*alikati ... dinuhos*
drinking water	*khaane paani*
rice	*bhaat*
soup	*jhol*

Please give me ...	*malaai ... dinuhos*
cold beer	*chiso bir*
a meal	*khaanaa*

I cannot eat ...	*ma ... khaana sakdina*
meat	*maasu*
spicy food	*piro*

What is this/that?	*yo/tyo ke ho?*
I am hungry/thirsty.	*malaai bhok/tirkhaa laagyo*
How do you like the food?	*khaanaa kasto laagyo?*
The meal was delicious.	*khaanaa mitho laagyo*
The food isn't hot.	*khaanaa tato chhaina*
Please bring me ...	*malaai ... leraaunuhos*

I am a vegetarian.	*ma saakaahaari hŭ*
I don't eat ...	*ma ... khaandina*
meat	*maasu*
fish	*maachhaa*
dairy products	*dugdhashaalaako khaanaa*

Meat

Maasu

buff (water buffalo)	*raãgako maasu*
chicken	*kukhuraako maasu*
dried fish	*sukeko maachhaa*
eel	*baam*
fish	*maachhaa*
goat	*khasiko maasu*
liver	*kalejoko maasu*
pork	*sŭgurko maasu*
yak meat	*chaũrigaaiko maasu*

Vegetables

Tarkaari

beans	*simi*
cabbage	*bandaakobi*
carrot	*gaajar*
cauliflower	*kaauli*
chilli pepper	*khorsaani*
choko squash	*iskus*

corn	*makai*
cucumber	*kaãkro*
eggplant	*bhaantaa*
garlic	*lasun*
green pepper	*bhēdaa khursaani*
leafy vegetables	*saagpaat*
lettuce	*jiriko saag*
mushroom	*chyaau*
onion	*pyaaj*
parsley	*jvangko saag*
peas	*keraau*
potato	*aalu*
pumpkin	*pharsi*
radish	*mulaa*
spinach	*paalungo*
squash	*laukaa, ghiraũlo, karelo*
sweet potato	*sakharkhanda*
tomato	*golbhēdaa*
turnip	*salgam*
yam	*tarul*

Cereals & Legumes   *Annaharu*

barley, oats	*jau*
broad beans	*bakulaa*
lentils – black	*kaalo daal*
lentils – brown	*khairo daal*
lentils – red	*masur daal*
millet	*kodo*
rice – unhusked	*dhaan*
rice – uncooked	*chaamal*
rice – cooked	*bhaat*

soybeans	*bhatmaas*
wheat	*gahū*

Fruit — Phalphul

apple	*syaau*
apricot	*khurpaani*
banana	*keraa*
cherry	*paiyūkhaalko phal*
coconut	*nariwal*
dates	*chhohoraa*
fig	*anjir*
grape	*angur*
grapefruit	*bhogate*
guava	*ambaa*
lemon	*kaagati*
mandarin	*suntalaa*
mango	*aāp*
melon	*tarbujaa*
orange	*suntalaa*

papaya	*mewaa*
peach	*aaru*
pear	*naaspaati*
pineapple	*bhuĩkatahar*
plum	*aarubakhadaa*
pomegranate	*anaar*
raisin	*daakh*
sweet lime	*mosam*

Dairy Products — Dugdhashaalaako Khaanaa

butter	*makkhan*
cheese	*chij*
cream	*tar*
ghee	*ghiu*
ice cream	*khuwaa baraph*
milk	*dudh*
yoghurt (curd)	*dahi*

Bread — Roti

biscuit, cookie	*biskut*
bread – flat	*chapaati, puri*
bread – loaf	*pauroti*
flour	*pitho*

Nuts — Supaari

almond	*kaagati baadaam*
cashew	*kaaju*
walnut	*okhar*
peanut	*badaam*

Herbs, Spices & Other Condiments	Jadibutiharu, Masalaaharu
basil	tulasi
cardamom	sukmel
cinnamon	daalchini
cloves	lwaan
coriander	dhaniyaā
chilli	khorsaani
coriander – fresh	hariyo dhaniyaā
cumin	jiraa
fennel	soph
fenugreek	methi
ginger	aduwaa
honey	maha
mustard	raayo
mustard – oil	raayoko tel
mustard – seed	raayoko biu
nutmeg	jaaiphal
oil	tel
pepper	marich
pickle, relish	achaar
saffron	keshar
salt	nun
seed	biu
sesame seeds	tilko biu
sugar	chini
sugar cane	ukhu
tamarind	amili
turmeric	besaar
vinegar	sirkaa

Drinks

alcohol	*raksi*
beer	*bir*
beer – millet	*tumbaa*
beer – rice	*chyaang, jaãd*
black coffee	*kaalo kaphi*
juice	*ras*
lemon tea	*kaagati chiyaa*
milk coffee	*dudh kaphi*
water	*paani*
boiled water	*umaaleko paani*

Some Useful Words

bitter	*tito*
cold	*chiso*
to cook	*pakaaunu*
delicious	*mitho*
empty	*khaali*
to feed	*khuwaaunu*
fresh	*taajaa*
fried	*bhuteko*
hot	*tato*
kitchen	*bhaanchha*
raw, unripe	*kaãcho*
ripe, cooked	*paakeko*
salty	*nunilo*
sour	*amilo*
spicy	*piro*
stale	*baasi*
sweet	*guliyo*

Table Articles

cup	*kap*
dish, utensil	*bhaã̃daa*
fork	*kaãtaa*
glass	*gilaas*
jug	*surahi*
knife	*chakku*
napkin	*rumaal*
plate	*thaal*
spoon	*chamchaa*
toothpick	*sinko*

a cup of ...	*ek kap ...*
a glass of ...	*ek gilaas ...*
a packet of ...	*ek poko ...*

Some Useful Phrases

Where was this cheese made?	*yo chij kahaã baneko ho?*
What kind of milk is it made from?	*kun dudhbaata baneko ho?*
Yak milk.	*chaũrigaaiko dudhbaata*
Where can you get this kind of cheese in Kathmandu?	*yasto chij kaathmaadaũmaa kahaã paainchha?*
How much per kg?	*ek kiloko kati parchha?*
Do you like beer?	*tapaaĩlaai bir manparchha?*
Yes/No.	*man parchha/pardaina*
What do you like?	*tapaaĩlaai ke manparchha?*
Would you like tea or coffee?	*tapaaĩlaai chiyaa ki kaphi?*
I'd like coffee.	*malaai kaphi*

Shopping

In Kathmandu and other towns, most shopkeepers speak some English, but outside the more populated areas this is not necessarily the case. To address a shopkeeper, follow the suggestions in the Greetings & Civilities chapter. He or she may respond with 'speak', *bhannuhos*. Remember that 'please' and 'thank you' are not necessary. Just state what you want and add 'please give', *dinuhos*. Generally, bargaining is not appropriate for basic household goods or foodstuffs.

Nepalese currency is the rupee, *rupaiyaā*, divided into 100 *paisaa*, which is also the word for 'money'. A 25-paisa coin is called a *sukaa*, and a 50-paisa coin is a *mohar*. Small prices are often quoted in sukas and mohars rather than rupees, so a 75-paisa item will be three sukas.

Excuse me, shopkeeper.	*saahuji*
Yes, can I help you?	*hajur, bhannuhos*
Please give me a needle and thread.	*malaai siyo ra dhaago dinuhos*
Here you are.	*linuhos*
How much is that?	*kati bhayo?*
75 paisa.	*tin sukaa*
Where is the nearest ...?	*najikai ... kahaā chha?*
bank	*baīk*
barber	*hajam*
bookshop	*kitaab pasal*
clothing store	*lugaa pasal*
cobbler	*saarki*

laundry	*lugaadhune thaaũ*
market	*bajaar*
pharmacy	*ausadhi pasal*
shoeshop	*juttaa pasal*
teashop	*chiyaa pasal*
vegetable shop	*tarkaari pasal*

I'd like to buy a ...	*... kinna man laagchha*
I'm just looking.	*herdaichhu*
How much is this pen?	*yo kalamko kati paisaa ho?*
That's expensive!	*mahãgo chha!*
It's cheap!	*sasto chha!*
How much do eggs cost?	*phulko kati ho?*
Twenty-five paisa each.	*eutako ek sukaa*

Where can I buy ...?	*... kahaã paainchha?*
paper	*kaagaj*
soap	*saabun*
string	*dori*

Do you have a ...?	*tapaaĩkahaã ... chha?*
hat	*topi*
newspaper	*akhabaar*
pencil	*sisaakalam*

Bargaining

In Nepal it is customary to bargain, *moltol garnu*, especially for tourist items. As in most Asian countries, it is a way of life, and foreigners are presumed wealthier than locals. With a little patience and goodwill, you will be able to reduce the price of most items to the satisfaction of both yourself and the shopkeeper. Tibet

is one of the few places where bargaining is not the norm, but this attitude changes dramatically when Tibetans trade in Nepal!

Do you have Tibetan dresses?	*tapaaīkahaā chubaa chha?*
Yes, have a look.	*chha, hernuhos*
How much is this one?	*yasko kati parchha?*
Three hundred rupees.	*tin say rupaiyaā*
That's expensive.	*mahāgo bhayo*
I don't have that much money.	*masāga teti paisaa chhaina*
Could you lower the price?	*alikati ghataaunu hunchha ki?*
I'll give 200 rupees.	*dui say rupaiyaā dinchhu*
That's not possible, give me 250.	*hūdaina, dui say pachaas dinuhos*
OK.	*hunchha*
No, I don't want it.	*chaahindaina*

Souvenirs   *Chino*

brassware	*pitalko saamaan*
carpet	*galaīchaa*
earring	*tap*
(a pair of) earrings	*ek jodaa tap*
embroidery	*buttaa*
gem, jewel	*juhaaraat*
gold	*sun*
handicraft	*hastakalaa*
incense burner	*dhup dani*
jewellery	*gahanaa*
mask	*makundo*
necklace	*maalaa*

Nepalese knife	*khukuri*
ornament	*gahanaa*
painting	*chitra, thangka*
pottery	*maatoko saamaan*
ring	*aūthi*
silver	*chaãdi*
statue	*murti*
wooden article	*kaathbaata baneko bastu*

Clothing / *Lugaaharu*

belt	*peti*
button	*taāk*
cap, hat	*topi*
cloth	*kapadaa*
coat	*kot*
dress, frock	*jaamaa*
gloves	*panjaa*
to get dressed	*lugaa lagaaunu*
shirt	*kamij*
shoes	*juttaa*

socks	*mojaa*
sandals	*chappal*
shorts, underpants	**kattu**
T-shirt, vest	*ganji*
waistcoat	*istakot*

Nepalese national dress is a sari, *saari*, and blouse, *cholo*, for women, and a tunic, *daauraa*, and trousers, *suruwaal*, for men.

| Can I try it on? | *lagaai herna hunchha?* |
| It fits well/doesn't fit. | **thik chha/chhaina** |

It is too ...	*dherai ... chha*
big/small	**thulo/saano**
short/long	**chhoto/laamo**
tight/loose	**kasinchha/khukulo**

| Can you make it in my size? | *malaai euta lugaa banaai dinu sakinchha?* |

Materials

cotton	*suti*
handmade	*haatle baneko*
leather	*chhaalaa*
silk	*resham*
wool	*un*

Colours   *Rangharu*

black	*kaalo*
blue	*nilo*
bright	*chahakilo*

brown	*khairo*
dark	*ādhyaaro*
green	*hariyo*
light	*ujyaalo*
multicoloured	*rangi*
orange	*suntalaa rang*
pale	*phikkaa*
pink	*gulaaphi*
purple	*pyaaji*
red	*raato*
white	*seto*
yellow	*pahēlo*

Toiletries

to brush/comb hair	*kapaal kornu*
to brush teeth	*daāt maajhnu*
comb	*kaaīyo*
condom	*thaal*
hairbrush	*kapaal korne*
laxative	*julaaph*
razorblade	*patti*
shampoo	*dhulaai*
to shave	*khauranu*
soap	*saabun*
toothbrush	*daāt maajhne burus*

Stationery & Publications
Chitthi Patralaai Chaahine Saamaan

aerogram	*hawaaipatra*
airmail	*hawaaidaak*
book	*kitaab*

dictionary	*shabdakosh*
envelope	*khaam*
exercise book	*kaapi*
ink	*masi*
ledgerpad	*khaataa*
letterpad	*chitthi lekhne kaapi*
magazine	*patrapatrikaa*
map	*naksaa*
newspaper	*akhabaar*
novel	*upanyaas*
paper	*kaagaj*
pen	*kalam*
pencil	*sisaakalam*
safety pin	*huk*
scissors	*kaĩchi*
stamp	*tikat*
writing pad	*lekhne kaapi*

Photography   *Tasbir Khichne Kalaa*

Please give me a film for this camera.	*yasko kyaameraalaai euta ril dinuhos*
How much is it for developing?	*ek ril print garnu, kati paisaa laagchha?*
When will it be ready?	*kahile aaune?*
Do you fix cameras?	*kyaameraa banaaunu hunchha?*

colour film	*rangin ril*
B&W film	*kaalo seto ril*

Smoking   *Dhumrapaan*

cigarette	*churot*

hashish	*chares*
hemp	*bhang*
hookah	*hukkaa*
marijuana	*gaãjaa*
matches	*salaai*
pipe	*churot paip*
tobacco	*surti*

A packet of cigarettes, please. *ek battaa churot dinuhos*
Do you have a light? *salaai chha?*

Weights & Measures

The metric system is in common use, but there are some measures
particular to Nepal, approximating the following:

| ½ kg/litre | *maanaa* |
| handful | *muthi* |

  ½ muthi = one chauthai
  four chauthai = one maanaa

| 200 grams | *paau* |
| 800 grams | *ser* |

| metre | *gaj* |

| span | *bitto* |

  four bitto = one gaj

Size & Quantity

| enough | *prashasta* |
| heavy | *gahraü* |

less	*ajha kamti*
light	*halukaa*
a little bit	*alikati*
long	*laamo*
(too) many, much	*dherai*
more	*ajha dherai*
short	*chhoto*
some	*kehi, kunai*
tall	*aglo*
too	*saahrai*

Some Useful Phrases

I would like to buy ...	*malaai ... kinna man laagchha*
Do you have others?	*arko kunai chha?*
I do/don't like it.	*malaai man parchha/pardaina*
May I see it?	*heraũ*
I'll take it.	*linchhu*
There is none.	*chhaina*
Which one? This one?	*kun chaahĩ? yo?*
Show it to me.	*dekhaaunuhos*
Can you show me the price?	*mol dekhaaunuhos*
Do you accept credit cards?	*credit card hunchha?*
What is it made of?	*kele baneko?*
Where was it made?	*kahaã baneko?*
What else do you need?	*aru kehi chaahinchha ki?*
That's all, how much is it?	*teti maatrai, kati bhayo?*
Is your carpet old or new?	*tapaaĩko galaĩchaa nayaã ho ki puraano?*
Where is the weekly market?	*haat bajaar kahaã chha?*
When is the weekly market?	*haat bajaar kahile hunchha?*

Some Useful Words

available	*paainchha*
bag, pack	*jholaa*
basket	*tokari*
battery	*masalaa*
bottle	*sisi*
box	*baakas*
bucket	*baaltin*
to buy	*kinnu*
carrybasket	*doko*
cheap	*sasto*
to choose	*chhaannu*
expensive	*mahãgo*
mat	*gundri*
mirror	*ainaa*
needle	*siyo*
new	*nayaã*
old	*puraano*
packet	*poko, battaa*
receipt	*bil*
to repair	*marmat garnu*
to serve	*sewaa garnu*
to sew	*siunu*
shop	*pasal*
to spend	*kharcha garnu*
string, rope	*dori*
thread	*dhaago*
total	*jammaa*
umbrella	*chhaataa*

Health

It is a good idea to be vaccinated against various diseases such as typhoid, tetanus and meningitis before going to Nepal. If you forget this worthwhile precaution, the Bir Hospital in Kathmandu does some inoculations. You should also take some antimalarial drugs if you're planning to go into the southern jungles, and remember that, with most antimalarial treatments, you'll need to start taking them two weeks prior to being in the area.

Never drink tap or river water unless it has been boiled and preferably also filtered, and insist on being served only properly sterilised water. Water that has only been filtered is still unsafe to drink. Water purification tablets are useless against Nepal's water-borne amoebae, and only iodine is effective. Bottled water is widely available and quite cheap. If you are unlucky enough to become sick, Kathmandu has good medical facilities, as do some other places. But if you have an accident or fall ill while trekking, you may need some help reaching a doctor. Nepalese pharmacies stock a wide range of Western medicines, available without prescription, and they give helpful advice. Traditional Ayurvedic medicines from plants are also prepared in Nepal, and Tibetan medicines are another alternative.

I am sick.	*ma biraami chhu*
I need a doctor.	*daaktarlaai jãchaaunu parchha*
Where can I find a good doctor?	*raamro daaktar kahaã chha?*
Please call a doctor.	*daaktarlaai bolaaunuhos*
I want a female doctor.	*malaai keti daaktar chaahiyo*

Where is the/a …?	… kahaã chha?
chemist	ausadhi pasal
dentist	daãtko **daak**tar
health post/clinic	chikitsaalaya
hospital	aspataal

Where is the nearest hospital?	najikai aspataal kahaã chha?
I need a porter.	malaai bhariyaa chaahinchha
Please carry me to …	… samma malaai boknuhos
Please send a message.	khabar pathaaunuhos

Complaints

My … hurts	mero … dukhyo
eye	aãkhaa
head	**t**aauko
stomach	pet
tooth	daãt

He/She broke his/her …	wahaãko … bhaãchyo
ankle	goli gaã**t**ho
arm	paakhuraa
leg	khuttaa

It hurts here.	yahaã dukhchha
I feel dizzy/weak.	malaai ringataa/kamjor laagyo
I've been bitten.	malaai **t**okyo
I'm having trouble breathing.	saas pherna sakdina
I've been vomiting.	baantaa garẽ
I can't sleep.	sutna sakdina
I can't move my …	mero … chalaauna sakdina

| I'm allergic to ... | *malaai ... linu hūdaina* |
| that | *tyo ausadhi* |

Please give me ...	*malaai ... dinuhos*
aspirin	*aaisprin*
bandages	*patti*
iodine	*aaidin*
medicine	*ausadhi*

I have ...	*malaai ... laagyo*
altitude sickness	*uchchaai, lekh*
asthma	*damko byathaa*
constipation	*dishaa banda*
a cold	*sardi, rughaa*
a cough	*khoki*
cramp	*baūdyaai*
a cut/wound	*ghaau*
dehydration	*paani sukaauna*
diarrhoea	*jhaadaa*
dysentery	*ragat maasi*
fever	*jwaro*
food poisoning	*khaanaa kharaab*
frostbite	*tusaarole khaeko*
indigestion	*apach*
an infection	*rog sarna*
an inflammation	*sunnieko abasthaa*
influenza	*rughaa-khokiko jwaro*
an itch	*chilaauna*
cholera	*haijaa*
diabetes	*madhumeha*
epilepsy	*chhaare rog*

malaria	*aulo*
meningitis	*gidiko jaalo sunnine rog*
mucus	*kaph*
a pain	*dukhaai*
a rash	*raatopan*
arthritis	*baath*
a sprain	*markaai*
a sore throat	*ghaāti dukheko*
typhoid	**taaiphaaid**
venereal disease	*bhiringi*
worms	*jukaa*

I burned my ...	*mero ... maa polyo*
I need something for ...	*malaai ... dukheko, kunai ausadhi dinuhos*
I haven't menstruated for ...	*rajaswalaa bhayo chhaina ... samma*

How many times a day?	*dinko kati patak?*
Is there a good dentist (here)?	*raamro daātko daaktar chha?*
I have a toothache.	*mero daāt dukheko chha*
Please give me anaesthetic.	*nishchetak dinuhos*
I have been vaccinated.	*sui liisakē*
I have my own syringe.	*masāga aaphno siyo chha*

Some Useful Phrases

How are you?	*tapaaīlaai sanchai chha?*
Not good.	*ali ali sanchai chhaina*
What's the matter?	*ke bhayo?*
I have a headache.	*mero kapaal dukhyo*

When did your headache start?	*kahile dekhi kapaal dukheko?*
Have you eaten?	*khaanaa khaanu bhayo?*
Did you take any medicine?	*ausadhi khaanu bhayo?*
I'm feeling fine now.	*ahile thik bhayo*

Body Parts

ankle	*goli gaātho*
appendix	*parishista*
arm	*paakhuraa*
back	*pithū*
backbone	**dhaad**
blood	*ragat*
body	*sharir, jiu*
bone	**haad**
brain	*gidi*
breast	*stan*
buttock	*chaak*
cheek	*gaalaa*
chest	*chhaati*
ear	*kaan*
elbow	*kuhino*
eye	*aākhaa*
face	*mukh*
finger	*aūlaa*
foot	*paau*
hair	*kapaal, kesh*
hand	*haat*
head	*taauko, kapaal*
heart	*mutu*
hip	*nitamba*

joint	*jorni*
kidney	*mrigaulaa*
knee	*ghū**d**aa*
leg	*khu**tt**aa*
lips	*ōth*
liver	*kalejo*
lung	*phokso*
mouth	*mukh*
muscle	*maamshapeshi*
nails	*nang*
nape of neck	*gardhan*
neck	*ghaāti*
nose	*naak*
rib	*karang*
shoulder	*kaādh*
skin	*chhaalaa*
stomach	*pet*
teeth	*daāt*
throat	*ghaāti*
tongue	*jibro*

Some Useful Words

accident	*durghatanaa*
ache (v)	*dukhnu*
addiction	*tat, aasakti*
bleed (v)	*ragat aaunu*
blood pressure	*rakta chaap*
contraceptive	*garbhanirodhak*
disease	*rog*
faeces	*dishaa*
injection	*sui*

itch	*chilchilaahat*
leprosy	*kusta rog*
menstruation	*rajaswalaa*
nausea	*waakwaaki*
ointment	*malam*
oxygen	*praanbaayu*
pug	*pip*
recover (v)	*niko hunu*
sickness	*rog*
test	*jaāch*
tetanus	*dhanu rog*
urine	*pisaab*
vitamin	*bhitaamin*
vomit (v)	*baantaa garnu*

Hill ambulance service

Time, Dates & Festivals

Telling the Time

time	*samay*

What time is it?	*kati bajyo?*
At what time?	*kati bajetira?*
It is two o'clock.	*dui bajyo*
At two o'clock.	*dui baje*
By my watch it is two o'clock.	*mero ghadimaa dui bajyo*

plus a quarter	*sawaa*
plus a half	*saadhe*
minus a quarter	*paune*

a quarter to two (1.45)	*paune dui bajyo*
a quarter past two (2.15)	*sawaa dui bajyo*
2.30	*saadhe dui bajyo*
at about two o'clock in the morning	*bihaana dui bajetira*
two o'clock this evening	*aaja belukaa dui baje*
two o'clock exactly	*thik dui bajyo*

in the morning	*bihaana*
in the afternoon	*diũso*
in the evening	*belukaa*
at night	*raati*

Days of the Week

What day is it today?	*aaja ke baar?*

Monday	*sombaar*
Tuesday	*mangalbaar*
Wednesday	*budhbaar*
Thursday	*bihibaar*
Friday	*sukrabaar*
Saturday	*sanibaar*
Sunday	*aitbaar*

The Nepalese Calendar

In Nepal the Hindu calendar, Vikram Samvat, is in general use, although in India it is kept for ritual purposes. It is a lunar-solar system 57 years ahead of the Gregorian calendar, so that 1992 AD is 2049 VS. Both have 365 days and 12 months, but the number of days in a Nepalese month varies from 29 to 32. The first Nepalese month begins in mid-April. There are three other calendars which are less widely used: the Shakya Samvat used for astrology, the Newar Samvat of the Kathmandu Valley, and the Tibetan calendar.

mid-April – mid-May	*baisaakh*
mid-May – mid-June	*jeth*
mid-June – mid-July	*asaar*
mid-July – mid-August	*saaun*
mid-Aug – mid-Sept	*bhadau*
mid-Sept – mid-Oct	*asoj*
mid-Oct – mid-Nov	*kaartik*
mid-Nov – mid-Dec	*mangsir*
mid-Dec – mid-Jan	*pus*

mid-Jan – mid-Feb	*maagh*
mid-Feb – mid-March	*phaagun*
mid-March – mid-April	*chait*

When referring to the Vikram calendar, *gate* is used to indicate the date:

What is the date today?	*aaja kati gate?*
The first.	*ek gate*

The Gregorian calendar, *isavi san*, uses the word *taarikh* to indicate the date. Both *gate* and *taarikh* follow the number:

What is the date today?	*aaja kati taarikh?*
The third.	*tin taarikh*

Present **Bartamaan Samaya**

today	*aaja*
this week	*yo haptaa*
this morning	*aaja bihaana*
this month	*yo mahinaa*
this evening	*aaja belukaa*
this year	*yo barsa*
tonight	*aaja raati*
now	*ahile*

Past **Bhutkaal**

yesterday	*hijo*
yesterday morning	*hijo bihaana*
the day before yesterday, the other day	*asti*
last night	*hijo raati*

| last week | *gaeko haptaa* |
| last Friday | *gaeko sukrabaar* |

Future — **Bhabisya**

tomorrow	*bholi*
tomorrow night	*bholi raati*
the day after tomorrow	*parsi*
next week	*arko haptaa*
next month	*arko mahinaa*
coming year	*aaune barsa*

Some Useful Words

after	*pachhi*
afternoon	*diũso*
all day	*dinbhari*
always	*sadhaĩ*
before	*aghi*
century	*shataavdi*
dawn	*bihaana saberai*
day	*din*
dusk	*sandhyaakaal*
early	*saberai*
evening	*belukaa*
every day	*harek din*
five years ago	*paãch barsa bhayo*
fortnight	*pandhra din*
hour	*ghantaa*
late	**d**hilo
long ago	*dherai samay bhayo*
midnight	*madhyaraat*
minute	*minat*

month	*mahinaa*
morning	*bihaana*
never	*kahile hoina*
night	*raati*
noon	*madhyaanha*
nowadays	*achel*
recently	*haalsaalai*
sometimes	*kahile kahi*
soon	*chaãdai*
week	*haptaa*
a while ago	*ekai chhin bhayo*
year	*barsa, saal*

Some Useful Phrases

When did you come to Nepal?	*tapaaĩ nepaalmaa kahile aaunubhaeko?*
Two weeks ago.	*dui haptaa bhayo*
How long will you stay?	*kati basne?*
I will stay in Nepal for two years.	*ma nepaalmaa dui barsa baschhu*
What month is this?	*yo mahinaa kun ho?*
I'm going to Pokhara for three weeks.	*ma tin haptaakolaagi pokhaaramaa janchhu*

Festivals

There are many gods and related beings in Nepal, and over 50 festivals are celebrated every year. The official religion is Hinduism, but it mingles harmoniously with Buddhism, and many religious festivals are celebrated together by Hindus and Buddhists. Festivals are dated according to the ancient lunar calendar and fall on days relative to full or new moons.

Most temples are dedicated to one or other of a multitude of gods, each known in countless forms and under many names. (There are said to be 300 million Hindu deities!) Religion is a significant part of Nepalese culture, and you will find it easier to gain some understanding of the culture if you are familiar with religious terminology. Some of the most useful terms relating to religion and festivals are given below.

Festivals

Basant Panchami – Jan/Feb
  celebration of spring, in honour of Saraswati, the goddess of learning
Bisket Jatra – April
  feast of the death of the Snake Demons. Part of the Nepalese New Year.
Buddha Jayanti – April/May
  Buddha's birthday
Chaitra Dasain – March/April
  festival dedicated to Durga, exactly six months before the major Dasain
Dasain (Durga Puja) – Sept/Oct
  Nepal's biggest annual festival, celebrated in honour of Durga's slaying of the demons. On the Eighth Day of Dasain, sacrifices and offerings to Durga begin. *Navami* is the ninth day of Dasain and the main sacrifice day, on which all the Nepalese eat meat. *Vijaya Dashami* is the 10th day of Dasain, a family celebration.
Dipavali – Oct/Nov
  Festival of Lights. Third and most important day of Tihar, dedicated to Laxmi.

Gunla – Aug/Sept
  special month of Buddhist ceremonies
Holi – Feb/Mar
  Festival of Colours
Indra Jatra – Sept
  festival honouring Indra
Kartikkaya Purnimaa – Sept/Oct
  full moon day marking the end of Dasain. Celebrated by gambling.
Krishna Jayanti – Aug/Sept
  Lord Krishna's birthday, also known as Krishnasthami
Kumarsasthi – May/June
  birthday of Kartikkaya, also called Sithinakha
Losar – Feb/March
  two-week festival for Tibetan New Year
Mahalaxmi Puja – Nov
  harvest festival
Mani Rimdu – Nov
  three-day Sherpa festival, held at Thyangpoche Monastery in the Solu Khumbu region

Mani Rimdu performer

Mha Puja – Oct/Nov
  Newari New Year and day of self-worship
Naga Panchami – July/Aug
  day of the snake gods, who are rain-givers and guardians of
  water. Snakes are honoured.
Raksha Bhandhan – Aug
  Yellow thread given by priests on this day and worn for good
  luck up until Tihar or for at least a week; unlike sacred thread,
  available to women and foreigners
Rato Machhendranath Jatra – April/May
  Festival of Red Machhendranath, also known as Bhota Jatra,
  Festival of the Sacred Vest
Shivaratri – Feb
  Shiva's birthday
Tihar – Oct/Nov
  second-most important Hindu festival after Dasain, honouring
  certain animals on successive days. The third day is Dipavali.
Tij – Aug/Sept
  three-day Festival of Women

Gods & Prominent Beings
Bhairab
  destructive, fearsome form of Shiva.
Brahma
  Supreme Being of the Hindu Trinity, Great Creator of all
  worldly things. His consort is Saraswati, and his animal a swan
  or goose.
Buddha
  the Enlightened One; ninth incarnation of Vishnu

Durga
  wrathful, destructive form of Parvati, and killer of demons.
  Mahalaxmi is a form of Durga and one of the eight mother
  goddesses.
Ganesh
  elephant-headed god of wisdom, prosperity and success, and
  the remover of obstacles. Elder son of Shiva and Parvati, and
  easily the most popular god in Nepal. Also called *Vinayaka*.
  His animal is the shrew, a symbol of sagacity.
Garuda
  mythical man-bird, mount of Vishnu, hater of snakes
Green Tara
  Hindu/Buddhist goddess, spiritual consort of the *Dhyani
  Buddha*.
Hanuman
  monkey-faced god of the Ramayana. Trustworthy and alert, so
  often seen as a palace guard.
Indra
  Hindu king of the gods and god of rain. His vehicle is an
  elephant.
Jogini
  mystical goddess, counterpart of Bhairab, also known as *Blue
  Tara*
Kali
  terrifying form of Parvati and goddess of mysteries. The Black
  Goddess.
Kartikkaya
  younger son of Shiva and Parvati, and younger brother of
  Ganesh. Also known as *Kumar*, he is the god of war and
  commander of Shiva's army. His mount is a peacock.

Krishna
  eighth incarnation of Vishnu, a funloving cowherd and hero of the *Mahabharata*. His wife is *Radha*.

Laxmi
  goddess of wealth and prosperity, consort of Vishnu

Machhendranath
  Nepalese manifestation of *Avalokiteswara*, protector and god of rains and monsoon

Manjushri
  god of divine wisdom, founder of Nepalese civilisation and creator of the Kathmandu Valley

Parvati
  peaceful consort of Shiva, representing his female and, through Kali and Durga, his fearsome side. Her symbol is the yoni, complement to Shiva's lingam. *Mahadevi* is a form of Parvati.

Pashupati
  a benevolent form of Shiva. Lord of beasts and keeper of all living things; supreme god of Nepal.

Rama
  seventh incarnation of Vishnu and beloved hero of *Ramayana*. His wife is *Sita*.

Saraswati
  goddess of learning, intelligence and memory, and of the creative arts. Consort of Brahma, she rides a white swan and holds a bina.

Shakti
  female principle of Supreme Energy; as a god's consort, Shakti represents this side of his personality

Shiva
  second member of the Hindu Trinity. The destroyer and regenerator who represents time and procreation. The most

important god in Nepal, he is often represented by a lingam, his shakti is Parvati, his animal the bull *Nandi*, and his common symbols the trident and drum. His home is Mt Kailash in Tibet. He is supposed to smoke hashish. He takes various forms including Pashupati and Bhairab, and is supposed to have thousands of such manifestations. *Mahadev*, the great god, is also a manifestation of Shiva, and so is *Nataraj*, the god of cosmic dancing.

Surya
Hindu sun god, also worshipped as Narayan in Nepal, who rides a chariot drawn by seven or nine horses. In Buddhism, Surya is associated with the moon as a symbol of basic unity.

Taleju
goddess of the royal family, symbolised by flowers

Vaishnava
follower of Vishnu

Vishnu
third member of the Hindu trinity; the Preserver. Has appeared on earth in nine incarnations, with the tenth yet to come. His vehicle is the Garuda.

White Tara
consort of *Avalokiteswara*, protects humans while crossing the ocean of existence. Her symbol is a full-blown lotus.

Yama
king and judge of the dead. Crows are his messengers and so inauspicious.

Some Useful Words

aūsi, amavasya
the dark moon, a fortnight before the new moon

bahun
  Hindu priest, or Brahmin in Nepal

chaãdparba
  festival

chaitya
  small, lotusbud-shaped stupa

chirag
  ceremonial oil lamp or torch

deutaa
  god, goddess

devadut
  mother goddess

dhami
  medicine men from the Rai tribe, who are also spirit mediums
  and diviners

dharma
  religious teaching, law and doctrine defining the path to uni-
  versal harmony via individual morals

ghat
  riverside platform for cremation, and the name of any steps
  leading down to a river

guru
  spiritual guide who teaches by inspiring one to follow his
  example

jatra
  feast, festival procession

jayanti
  birthday celebration

jhankri
  hill-dwelling medicine man or faith healer, who performs in a
  trance while beating drums

jivan, jindagi
life
kal
death
karma
law of cause and effect: actions of all previous lives determine the soul's next rebirth
khat
canopied ceremonial palanquin for carrying idols
Kumari
young virgin girl, worshipped by the Nepalese as a living goddess
lama
spiritual teacher, religious instructor
Lamaism
Tibetan Tantric Buddhism
lingam
phallic symbol of Shiva, commonly used to represent him in temples. A symbol of Shiva's creative role.
maani
stone carved with Buddhist prayers
mahaatmaa
saint
Mahabharata
Hindu epic of the battle between two families, featuring Krishna
mandala
mystic circular design used as a meditation device. A visual aid to concentration.
mandap
pavilion

mandir
Hindu temple
mantra
prayer, invocation, religious incantation, magic spell
mela
fair
moksha
spiritual salvation from the cyclic rebirths of reincarnation; Hindu equivalent of nirvana
nilotpala
blue half-closed lotus, the night lotus, symbol of the Green Tara. Also called *utpala*.
nirvana
the eventual aim of all Buddhists: the achievement of a state of enlightenment and spiritual peace via the annihilation of individuality and the end of misery and pain, which are caused by desires
paap
lotus of any colour except blue; the day lotus. To Hindus it is especially sacred as a symbol of purity of descent; to Buddhists it symbolises self-creation.
praarthanaa
prayer
prasad
food, sacred after being offered in pujaa
pujaa
prayer, worship, religious ceremony
pujaari
priest
purnimaa, purne
bright fortnight preceding full moon

Ramayana
  popular Hindu epic in which the princess Sita is abducted by
  the evil demon king *Rawana*. Rama and Hanuman destroy
  Rawana and rescue Sita.

rath
  temple chariot, vehicle of the gods

sadhu
  a Hindu ascetic on a spiritual search, usually a follower of Shiva
  carrying a trident

samsara
  Hindu cycle of transmigration and reincarnation

sangha
  order or community of Buddhist monks

Shaivite
  follower of Shiva

stupa
  Buddhist temple or sanctuary

swastika
  for Hindus, an auspicious sign of law (*swasti* means 'well-
  being'); for Buddhists, a symbol of the esoteric doctrine of the
  Buddha

tantra
  text which expounds esoteric psycho-sexual mystic philosophy
  which leads to enlightenment. A major influence on Nepalese
  Hinduism and Buddhism.

Tara
  the Hindu/Buddhist female principle in various forms

tika
  auspicious mark of red *sindur* paste, placed on the forehead
  during puja or festivals

vahana
   animal that acts as vehicle of Hindu god

vajra
   thunderbolt or diamond: symbol of Tantric Buddhism. Destroys ignorance and symbolises purity and indestructibility. Represents nirvana and is the male complement of the female principle ghanta.

vajracharya
   Buddhist Newar priest

yana
   way, path or vehicle to Buddhist enlightenment

yogi
   holy man

yoni
   symbol of Parvati. Platelike disc with drain representing the female sexual organ, often found in combination with a lingam and acting as a reservoir for offerings.

Numbers

Nepalese numbers are used for counting, telling the time, measurements and in expressions of age. When counting people or things in Nepali, special words called counters must be used between the number and the noun. The noun always stays singular. The counter for things is *wataa*, and for people *janaa*, but informally *wataa* is also used for people. Using these counters is not the same as saying 'two things', and you should just think of them as part of the number. It's a bit like saying 'two sheets of paper' or 'two slices of bread'. The system is regular after the number three, but the first two need to be learnt individually.

one	*ek*	one (thing)	*eutaa*
two	*dui*	two (things)	*duitaa*
three	*tin*	three (things)	*tin wataa* or *tintaa*
four	*chaar*	four (things)	*chaar wataa*
five	*paāch*	five (things)	*paāch wataa*
ten	*das*	ten (things)	*das wataa*
twenty	*bis*	twenty (things)	*bis wataa*

How many (things)?	*kati wataa?*
How many (people)?	*kati janaa?*

apple	*syaau*
two apples	*duitaa syaau*
tiger	*baagh*
five tigers	*paāch wataa baagh*
person	*maanchhe*
one person	*ek janaa maanchhe*

sister	*bahini*
three sisters	*tin janaa bahini*

To make a multiple, add *-palta* to the number:

twice	*duipalta*
three times	*tinpalta*

Fractions

¼	*paau*
⅓	*tihaai*
½	*aadhaa*
1¼	*dedh*
2½	*adhaai*

1 ?   2 ?   3 ?   4 ?   5 ?

6 ?   7 ?   8 ?   9 ?   10 ?

11 ?? 12 ?? 13 ?? 14 ?? 15 ??

16 ?? 17 ?? 18 ?? 19 ?? 20 ??

Cardinal Numbers

All the numbers from one to 100 have been listed, as the pattern is not as obvious as in English. Note that the Nepalese system is divided differently from English into hundreds *(say)*, thousands *(hajaar)*, hundred thousands *(laakh)* and ten millions *(karod)*.

0	sunya	24	chaubis
1	ek	25	pachchis
2	dui	26	chhabbis
3	tin	27	sattaais
4	chaar	28	atthaais
5	paāch	29	unantis
6	chha	30	tis
7	saat	31	ektis
8	aath	32	battis
9	nau	33	tettis
10	das	34	chaūtis
11	eghaara	35	paītis
12	baarha	36	chhattis
13	terha	37	saītis
14	chaudha	38	athtis
15	pandhra	39	unanchaalis
16	sorha	40	chaalis
17	satra	41	ekchaalis
18	athaara	42	bayaalis
19	unnaais	43	trichaalis
20	bis	44	chaubaalis
21	ekkaais	45	paītaalis
22	baais	46	chhayaalis
23	teis	47	satchaalis

48	*athchaalis*	79	*unaasi*
49	*unanchaas*	80	*asi*
50	*pachaas*	81	*ekaasi*
51	*ekaaunna*	82	*bayaasi*
52	*baaunna*	83	*triyaasi*
53	*tripanna*	84	*chauraasi*
54	*chaubanna*	85	*pachaasi*
55	*pachpanna*	86	*chhayaasi*
56	*chhapanna*	87	*sataasi*
57	*sataaunna*	88	*athaasi*
58	*athaaunna*	89	*unaannabbe*
59	*unsatthi*	90	*nabbe*
60	*saathi*	91	*ekaannabbe*
61	*eksatthi*	92	*bayaannabbe*
62	*bayasatthi*	93	*triyaannabbe*
63	*trisatthi*	94	*chauraannabbe*
64	*chausatthi*	95	*pachaannabbe*
65	*paīsatthi*	96	*chhayaannabbe*
66	*chhayasatthi*	97	*santaannabbe*
67	*satasatthi*	98	*anthaannabbe*
68	*athsatthi*	99	*unaansay*
69	*unhattar*	100	*ek say*
70	*sattari*	101	*ek say ek*
71	*ekhattar*	200	*dui say*
72	*bahattar*	1000	*ek hajaar*
73	*trihattar*	2000	*dui hajaar*
74	*chauhattar*	10 000	*das hajaar*
75	*pachhattar*	100 000	*ek laakh*
76	*chhayahattar*	200 000	*dui laakh*
77	*sathattar*	1000 000	*das laakh*
78	*athhattar*	10 000 000	*ek karod*

Ordinal Numbers

These are formed by adding *-aū* to the simple number. The first four are irregular, however, and must be learnt individually:

first	*pahila*
second	*dosra*
third	*tesra*
fourth	*chautho*
fifth	*paāchaū*
sixth	*chhataū*
seventh	*sataū*
eighth	*aathaū*
ninth	*naū*
tenth	*dasaū*
twentieth	*bisaū*

Vocabulary

A

able (to be) – *saknu*
about – *tira, jati, baare*
above – *maathi*
abroad – *bideshma*
accident – *durghatanaa*
ache (v) – *dukhnu*
across – *paari*
actor/artist – *kalaakaar*
addiction – *tat, aasakti*
address – *thegaanaa*
advice – *sallaaha*
aerogram – *hawaaipatra*
aeroplane – *hawaaijahaaj*
afraid (to be) – *daraaunu*
after – *pachhi*
afternoon – *diūso*
again – *pheri*
age – *umer*
agriculture – *khetipaati*
aid – *sahayog*
air – *haawaa*
air mail – *hawaaidaak*
alcohol – *raksi*
all – *sabai*
all day – *dinbhari*
almond – *kaagati baadaam*

alone – *eklaai*
along – *bhari*
altitude sickness – *uchchaai, lekh*
always – *sadhaī*
anaesthetic – *nishchetak*
ancient – *praachin*
and – *ra/ani*
and then, and so – *ani*
angel – *devadut*
angry – *ris*
angry (to be) – *risaaunu*
animal – *janaawar*
ankle – *goli gaātho*
annoyed – *dikka*
answer (v) – *uttar*
ant – *kamilaa*
anyone – *kohi*
anything – *kehi*
apartment – *deraa*
appendix – *parishista*
apple – *syaau*
apricot – *khurpaani*
architect – *silpakar*
argument – *bahas*
arm – *paakhuraa*
arrive – *pugnu*
art – *kalaa*

117

arthritis – *baath*
artist/actor – *kalaakaar*
ask – *sodhnu*
ask for – *maagnu*
aspirin – *aaisprin*
asthma – *damko byathaa*
at – *maa*
autorickshaw – *tyaampu*
autumn – *sharadritu*
available – *paainchha*
available (to be) – *paaunu*

B

baby – *bachchaa*
baby's bottle – *dudh khuwaaune sisi*
back – *pithū*
backbone – **dhaad**
bad – *naraamro,kharaab*
bag/pack – *jholaa, thailo*
balcony – *baardali*
ball – *bhakundo*
banana – *keraa*
bandage – *patti*
bank – *baīk*
barber – *hajam*
bargain (v) – *moltol garnu*
barley – *jau*
basil – *tulasi*
basket – **t**okari
bat – *chamero*

bathe (v) – *nuhaaunu*
battery – *masalaa*
be – *hunu*
bean – *simi*
bear – *bhaalu*
beard – *daahri*
beautiful – *raamro, sundar*
because – *kinabhane*
bed – *khaat*
bedding – *bichhaaunaa*
bee – *mauri*
beef – *gaaiko maasu*
beer – *bir*
 – rice – *chyaang,jaād*
 – millet – *tumbaa*
before – *aghi*
beggar – *maagne*
begin – *shuru garnu*
behind/back – *pachhaadi*
below – *tala*
belt – *peti*
beside – *chheumaa*
between – *bich*
bicycle – *saikal*
big – **t**hulo
bill – *bil*
bird – *charaa*
birthday – official – *jayanti*
 – personal – *janma din*
biscuit – *biskut*
bite (v) – **t**oknu
bitter – *tito*

black – *kaalo*
blanket – *kambal*
bleed – *ragat aaunu*
blessing – *aashik*
blind – *andho*
blizzard – *hiūko aādhi*
blood – *ragat*
blood pressure – *rakta chaap*
blouse – *cholo*
blue – *nilo*
boat – *dūgaa*
body – *sharir, jiu*
boiled water – *umaaleko
    paani*
bone – *haad*
book – *kitaab*
border – *simaanaa*
bored (to be) – *waakka hunu*
borrow – *saapat linu*
boss – *maalik*
bottle – *sisi*
box – *baakas*
brain – *gidi*
branch – *haāgaa*
brassware – *pitalko saamaan*
brave – *bahaadur*
bread – *roti*
    – flat – *chapaati, puri*
    – loaf – *pauroti*
break (v) – *bhaāchnu*
breakfast – *bihaanako
    khaanaa*

breast – *stan*
breathe – *saas phernu*
bribe – *ghus*
bridge – *pul*
bright – *chahakilo*
bring – *leraaunu*
broadbean – *bakulaa*
brother – elder – *daai, daajyu*
    – younger – *bhaai*
brothers – *daajyubhaai*
brown – *khairo*
brush – *burus*
brush (v) – hair – *kapaal kornu*
    – teeth – *daāt maajhnu*
bucket – *baaltin*
Buddhism – *buddha dharma*
buff meat – *raāgako maasu*
buffalo (f) – *bhaīsi*
    (m) – *raāga*
building – *bhawan*
burn (v) – *polnu*
bus – *bas*
bush – *jhaadi*
businessperson – *bepaari*
busy – *vyasta*
but – *tara*
butter – *makkhan*
butterfly – *putali*
button – *taāk*
buy (v) – *kinnu*
buzzard – *baaj*
by – *le*

C

cabbage – *bandaakobi*
Calcutta – *kalkattaa*
calendar – *samvat*
call (v) – *bolaaunu*
camera – *kyaameraa*
camp (v) – *shibir (garnu)*
cancel – *radda garnu*
candle – *mainbatti*
cap – **t**opi
car – *motar*
cardamom – *sukmel*
cards – *tash*
careful (to be) – *hos garnu*
carpet – *galaĭchaa*
carrot – *gaajar*
carry – *boknu*
carrybasket – **d**oko
cashew – *kaaju*
cat – *biraalo*
cauliflower – *kaauli*
cave – *guphaa*
centre – *bich*
century – *shataavdi*
cereal – *anna*
chair – *mech*
change (v) money – *saatnu*
cheap – *sasto*
check (v) – *jaãchaaunu*
cheek – *gaalaa*
cheese – *chij*

cherry – *paiyũkhaalko phal*
chest – *chhaati*
chicken – *kukhuraa*
chicken meat – *kukhuraako maasu*
child – *bachchaa*
children – own – *chhoraachori*
– general – *ketaketi*
chilli pepper – *khorsaani*
choko – *iskus*
cholera – *haijaa*
choose – *chhaannu*
Christian – *krishchiyan*
Christianity – *isaai dharma*
cigarette – *churot*
cinnamon – *daalchini*
citizen – *naagarik*
city – *shahar*
clean (v) – *saphaa (garnu)*
clerk – *kaarindaa*
climb (v) – *chadhnu*
clinic – *chikitsaalaya*
clock – *bhitte ghadi*
cloth – *kapadaa*
clothes – *lugaa*
close (v) – *banda garnu*
cloud – *baadal*
cloudy – *badli*
cloves – *lwaan*
coat – *kot*
cobbler – *saarki*
cockroach – *saãglo*

coconut – *nariwal*
coffee – *kaphi*
coin – *mudraa*
   – 25 paisa – *sukaa*
   – 50 paisa – *mohar*
cold – weather – *jaaḍo*
   – touch – *chiso*
cold (viral infection) – *sardi,
   rughaa*
collect – *lina aaunu*
colour – *rang*
comb – *kaaĩyo*
comb (v) hair – *kapaal kornu*
come – *aaunu*
communist – *saamyavaadi*
compassion – *karuna, upaya*
condom – *thaal*
confirm – *pakkaa garnu*
constipation – *dishaabanda*
contraceptive – *garbhanirodhak*
conversation – *kuraakaani*
cook – *bhaanse*
cook (v) – *pakaaunu*
cookie – *biskuṭ*
cool – *shital*
coriander– *dhaniyaã*
   – fresh – *hariyo dhaniyā*
corn – *makai*
corner – *kunaa*
corruption – *bhrasṭaachaar*
cotton – *suti*
cough – *khoki*

count (v) – *gannu*
country – *desh*
cow – *gaai*
cowshed – *goṭh*
cramp – *baũḍyaai*
crazy – *baulaahaa*
cream – *tar*
creek – *kholaa*
cremation – *daaha sāskaar*
crocodile – *gohi*
crop – *baali*
crow – *kaag*
crowd – *bhiḍ*
cucumber – *kaãkro*
cultivate (v) – *khanjot garnu*
cultural show – *saãskritik
   pradarshan*
culture – *sāskriti*
cumin – *jiraa*
cup – *kap*
cupboard – *daraaj*
curd – *dahi*
curtain – *pardaa*
customs – *bhansaar*
cut – *ghaau*

D

daily – *dinhū, dinbhari*
dairy – *dugdhashaalaai*
dance (v) – *naachnu*
dancer – *naachne maanchhe*

dark – *ādhyaaro*
dark moon – *aūsi*
date – *gate, taarikh*
dates – *chhohoraa*
daughter – *chhori*
dawn – *bihaana saberai*
day – *din, baar*
day after tomorrow – *parsi*
day before yesterday – *asti*
dead – *mareko*
deaf – *bahiro*
death – *kal*
decide – *nirnaya garnu*
deer – *mriga*
defecate (v) – *dishaa garnu*
dehydration – *paani sukaauna*
delayed – **d**hilo
Delhi – *dilli*
delicious – *mitho*
democracy – *prajaatantra*
dentist – *daātko* **d**aaktar
deny – *namaannu*
development – *bikaas*
diabetes – *madhumeha*
diarrhoea – *jhaa**d**aa*
dictionary – *shabdakosh*
die (v) – *marnu*
different – *pharak*
difficult – *gaahro*
dinner – *bhaat*
direction – *dishaa*
dirty – *phohor*

discover – *pattaa laaunu*
discrimination – *paksapaat*
disease – *rog*
dish – *bhaā**d**aa*
distance (3 km) – *kos*
dizzy – *ringataa*
do – *garnu*
doctor – **d**aaktar
dog – *kukur*
dome – *stupaa*
donkey – *gadhaa*
door – **d**hokaa
down – *tala*
downhill – *oraalo*
downward – *talatira*
dozen – *darjan*
dream – *sapanaa*
dress – *jaamaa*
dress (v) – *lugaa lagaaunu*
dried fish – *sukeko maachhaa*
drink (v) – *piunu*
drinking water – *khaane paani*
drive (v) – *haāknu*
drowsy – *ūg*
drug – *okhati*
drunk – *raksi*
duck – *haās*
dusk – *sandhyaakaal*
dust – *dhulo*
dysentery – *ragat maasi*

E

eagle – *chil*
ear – *kaan*
early – *saberai, chaãdai*
earn – *kamaaunu*
earring – **t**ap
earth – *prithvi*
earthquake – *bhuīchaalo*
east – *purba*
easy – *sajilo*
eat – *khaanu*
economy – *artha byabasthaa*
education – *shikshaa*
eel – *baam*
egg – *phul*
eggplant – *bhaantaa*
elbow – *kuhino*
elder brother's wife – *bhaaujyu*
election – *chunaau*
electricity – *bijuli*
elephant – *hatti*
else – *aru*
embarrassed – *lajjit*
embassy – *raajdutaavaas*
embroidery – *buttaa*
empty – *khaali*
energy – *shakti*
engineer – *injiniyar*
English – *āgreji*
enjoy – *aananda linu*
enough – *prashasta*

enough (to be) – *pugnu*
envelope – *khaam*
epilepsy – *chhaare rog*
evening – *belukaa*
every – *harek*
exactly – **t**hik
exercise book – *kaapi*
exhaust oneself (v) – *thakaaunu*
expect – *apekshaa garnu*
expensive – *mahãgo*
extend – *thapnu*
even (number) – *jor*
eye – *aākhaa*

F

face – *mukh*
factory – *kaarkhaanaa*
faeces – *dishaa*

fair – *mela*
faith – *vishwaas*
falcon – *baaj*
family – *paribaar*
fan – *pākhaa*
far – **taadhaa**
farm – *khetbaari*
farmer – *kisaan*
fast – *chito, chaādai*
fast (n) – *vrata*
fat – *moto*
father – *buwaa, baa*
feast – *jatra, bhoj*
feed (v) – *khuwaaunu*
feel like – *man laagnu*
fennel – *soph*
fenugreek – *methi*
festival – *chaadbaad, parba*
fever – *jwaro*
(a) few – *thorai*
field – *khet*
fig – *anjir*
fight – *ladaai garnu*
film (cinema) – *philam, sinemaa*
film (photographic)
  – colour – *rangin ril*
  – B&W – *kaalo seto ril*
fine – *sanchai, aaraamai*
finger – *aūlaa*
fingernails – *nang*
firewood – *daauraa*

first – *pahila*
fish – *maachhaa*
flea – *upiyaā*
flour – *pitho*
flower – *phul*
flu – *rughaa khokiko jwaro*
fly (n) – *jhīngaa*
fog – *kuiro*
food – *khaanaa*
food poisoning – *khaanaa kharaab*
foot – *paau*
(on) foot – *hīdera*
for – *kolaagi*
foreigner – *bideshi*
forest – *ban*
forever – *sadhaī*
forget – *birsanu*
forgive – *maph garnu*
fork – *kaātaa*
fortnight – *pandhra din*
fox – *phyaauro*
freedom – *swatantrataa*
freeze (v) – *jamnu*
fresh – *taajaa*
Friday – *sukrabaar*
fried – *bhuteko*
friend – *saathi*
friendly – *milansaar*
frock – *jaamaa*
frog – *bhyaaguto*
from (place) – *baata*

from (place, time) – *dekhi*
(in) front of – *agaadi*
frost – *tusaaro*
frostbite – *tusaarole khaeko*
fruit – *phalphul*
fun – *majaa*
future – *bhabisya*

G

game – *khel*
garbage – *mailaa*
garden – *bagaĭchaa*
garlic – *lasun*
gate – **d**hokaa
gem – *juhaaraat*
get dressed – *lugaa lagaaunu*
get off – *orlinu*
get up – *uthnu*
ghat – *ghaat*
ghee – *ghiu*
ginger – *aduwaa*
girl – *keti*
give – *dinu*
glass – *gilaas*
go – *jaanu*
go on foot – *hĭdera jaanu*
goat – *bokaa, khasi*
goatmeat – *khasiko maasu*
god, goddess – *deutaa*
gold – *sun*
good – *raamro, asal*

goodbye – *namaste, namaskaar*
goods – *saamaan*
good-tasting – *mitho*
government – *sarkaar*
grandfather – *baaje*
grandmother – *bajyai*
grape – *angur*
grapefruit – *bhogate*
grateful – *kritagya*
green – *hariyo*
green pepper – *bhēdaa khursaani*
Gregorian calendar – *isavi san*
guava – *ambaa*
guest – *paahunaa*
guesthouse – *paunaghar*
guide – *baato dekhaaune maanchhe*

H

hair – *kapaal, kesh*
hairbrush – *kapaalkorne burus*
hairpin – *kaātaa*
half – *aadhaa*
hand – *haat*
handicraft – *hastakalaa*
handkerchief – *rumaal*
handmade – *haatle baneko*
hanging bridge – *jhulunge pul*
happy – *khusi*

hashish – *chares*
hat – ***topi***
he – informal – *u,tyo,yo*
  – formal – *wahaā*
head – ***taauko, kapaal***
headstrap – *naamlo*
health post (clinic)
  – *chikitsaalaya*
heart – *mutu*
heaven – *swarga*
heavy – *gahraū*
hell – *narak*
hello – *namaste, namaskaar*
help (v) – *maddat garnu*
hemp – *bhang*
hen – *kukhuri*
herb – *ja***d***ibuti*
here – *yahaā*
high – *aglo, ucho*
hill – *pahaa***d***
hillperson – *pahaa***d***i*
Hindu calendar – *vikram samvat*
Hinduism – *hindu dharma*
hip – *nitamba*
hire – *bhaa***d***aamaa linu*
hole – *pwaal*
holiday – *bidaa*
holy – *pabitra*
homosexuality – *samalinga sambhogataa*
honest – *imaandaar*

honey – *maha*
hookah – *hukkaa*
horse – *gho***d***aa*
hospital – *aspataal*
hot – weather – *garmi*
  – touch – *tato*
hotel – *hotel*
hour – *ghantaa*
how – quality – *kasto*
  – means – *kasari*
how much/many – *kati*
human – *maanis*
humid – *vaaspiya*
hunger/hungry – *bhok*
hurry (v) – *chito garnu*
(in a) hurry – *hataar*
hurt – *chot*
hurt (v) – *dukhnu*
husband – own – *logne*
  – someone else's – *srimaan*
hut – *chhaapro, jhupro*

I

I – *ma*
ice – *baraph*
icecream – *khuwaa baraph*
ice peak – *himaal*
idea – *bichaar*
idol – *murti*
if – *yadi*
ill – *biraami*

illegal – *abaidh*
illness – *rog*
immediately – *turuntai*
in – *maa*
incense burner – *dhup dani*
including – *samet*
India – *hindustaan, bhaarat*
indigestion – *apach*
infection – *rog sarna*
inflammation – *sunnieko
    avasthaa*
influenza – *rughaa khokiko
    jwaro*
information – *khabar*
in front of – *agaadi*
injection – *sui*
injury – *chot*
ink – *masi*
inn – *bhatti*
insect – *kiraa*
intellect – *buddhi*
interesting – *chaakhlaagdo*
invite – *nimtaa garnu*
iodine – *aaidin*
Islam – *islaam dharma*
it – *tyo, yo*
itch (v) – *chilaaunu*

J

jackal – *syaal*
jail – *jhyaalkhaannaa*

Jew/Jewish – *yahudi*
jewel – *juhaaraat*
jewellery – *gahanaa*
job – *kaam*
joint – *jorni*
joke – *thattaa*
journalist – *patrakaar*
journey – *yaatraa*
Judaism – *yahudi dharma*
jug – *surahi, lotaa*
juice – *ras*
jump (to) – *uphranu*
jungle – *ban*

K

Kathmandu – *kaathmaadaũ*
keep going – *jaãdai garnu*
kerosene – *mattitel*
kidney – *mrigaulaa*
kill (v) – *maarnu*
kindness – *dayaa*
king – *raajaa*
kiss – *mwaai*
kitchen – *bhaanchha*
knee – *ghũdaa*
knife – *chakku, khukuri*
know (v) – person – *chinnu*
    – thing – *thaahaa paaunu*
knowledge – *bodhi, prajna*

L

lake – *taal*
lake (small) – *kund*
lamp/light – *batti*
lamp/torch (ceremonial) – *chirag*
lamp (sacred butter) – *dip*
landslide – *pairo*
language – *bhaasaa*
large – **thulo**
last – *antim, gaeko*
late – **dhilo**, *aberai*
laugh (v) – *haāsnu*
launder (v) – *dhunu*
laundry – *lugaadhune thaaū*
lawyer – *wakil*
laxative – *julaaph*
lazy – *alchi*
leaf – *paat*
leafy vegetables – *saagpaat*
learn (v) – *siknu*
leather – *chhaalaa*
leave – *chodnu*
leech – *jukaa*
left – *baayaā*
leg – *khuttaa*
legal – *kaanuni*
lemon – *kaagati*
lentils – *daal*
  – black – *kaal daal*
  – brown – *khairo daal*
  – red – *masur daal*

leopard – *chituwaa*
leper – *kusthi*
leprosy – *kusta rog*
letter – *chitthi*
letterpad – *chitthilekhne kaapi*
lettuce – *jiriko saag*
level – *samma*
library – *pustakaalaya*
(tell) lies (v) – **dhaātnu**
life – *jivan, jindagi*
lightbulb – *chim*
light (colour) – *ujyaalo*
lightning – *bijuli chamkaai*
lightweight – *halukaa*
like – *jasto*
like (v) – *man parnu*
lion – *sīha*
lips – *ōth*
listen – *sunnu*
a little (bit) – *ali ali, alikati*
live (v) – *basnu*
liver – *kalejo*
lizard – *chhepaaro*
load – *bhaari*
lock (v) – *taalchaa garnu*
lodge – *laaj*
long – *laamo*
look (v) – *hernu*
look after – *herbichaar garnu*
look for – *khojnu*
loose – *khukulo*
lose – *haraaunu*

lost – *haraauna*
loud – *thulo*
louse – *jumra*
love – *maayaa, prem*
low – *hocho*
lower – *ghataaunu*
lucky – *bhaagyamaani*
luggage – *saamaan*
lunch – *chamenaa*
lung – *phokso*

M

machine – *kal*
magazine – *patrapatrikaa*
make (v) – *banaaunu*
malaria – *aulo*
male – *bhaale*
mandarin – *suntalaa*
mango – *aāp*
many, much – *dherai*
map – *naksaa*
marijuana – *gaājaa*
market – *bajaar*
marriage – *bihaa*
marry – *bihaa garnu*
mask – *makundo*
mat – *gundri*
match (v) – *milnu*
matches – *salaai*
mattress – *dasanaa*
maybe – *shaayaad*

me – *malaai*
meal – *khaanaa*
measure – ½ kg/litre – *maanaa*
 – yard – *gaj*
 – 200 grams – *paau*
 – handful – *muthi*
 – ⅛ acre – *ropani*
meat – *maasu*
medicine – *ausadhi*
meet – *bhetnu*
melon – *tarbujaa*
melt – *pagaalnu*
meningitis – *gidiko jaalo
 sunnine rog*
menstruation – *rajaswalaa*
message – *khabar*
middle – *bich*
midnight – *madhyaraat*
milk – *dudh*
millet – *kodo*
minute – *minat*
mirror – *ainaa*
mistake – *galti*
mix (v) – *misaaunu*
moment – *ek chhin*
monastery – *gumbaa*
Monday – *sombaar*
money – *paisaa*
mongoose – *nyaauri musaa*
monkey – *baādar*
monsoon – *barsayukta
 haawaa*

month – *mahinaa*
monument – *smaarak*
moon (full) – *purnimaa*
moon (dark) – *aūsi, amavasya*
morning – *bihaana*
mosque – *masjid*
mosquito – *laamkhutte*
mother – *aamaa*
mountain – *himaal*
mountaineer – *parbataarohi*
mouse – *musaa*
mouth – *mukh*
move – *chalaaunu*
mucus – *kaph*
mud – *hilo*
multicoloured – *rangi*
muscle – *maamshapeshi*
museum – *samgrahaalaya*
mushroom – *chyaau*
music – *sāgit*
Muslim – *musalmaan*
mustard – oil – *raayoko tel*
  – seed – *raayoko biu*
mutton – *khasiko maasu*
my – *mero*

N

name – *naam*
napkin – *rumaal*
narrow – *saāghuro*
nature – *prakriti*

nausea – *waakwaaki*
near – *najik*
nearest – *najikai*
neck – *ghaāti*
necklace – *maalaa*
needed (to be) – *chaahinu*
needle – *siyo*
Nepal – *nepaal*
Nepalese knife – *khukuri*
net – *jaal*
never – *kahile hoina*
new – *nayaā*
news – *samaachaar*
newspaper – *akhabaar*
next – *arko, aaune*
night – *raat*
no – *āhā, hoina, chhaina*
noise – *aawaaj*
noisy – *hallaa*
noon – *madhyaanha*
no-one – *kohi (pani)*
north – *uttar*
nose – *naak*
notebook – *kaapi*
nothing – *kehi (pani)*
novel – *upanyaas*
now – *ahile*
nowadays – *achel*
number – *nambar, sankhyaa*
nurse – *parichaarikaa*
nut – *supaari*
nutmeg – *jaaiphal*

O

oats – *jau*
o'clock – *baje, bajyo*
odd (number) – *bijor*
of – *ko*
offend – *apamaan garnu*
office – *kaaryaalaya*
often – *aksar*
oh – *aoho, e, u*
oil – *tel*
ointment – *malam*
OK – *thikchha, hunchha, haas*
old (person) – *budha, budhi*
old (thing) – *puraano*
on – *maa*
once – *ekchoti*
on foot – *hīdera*
onion – *pyaaj*
only – *maatrai*
open (v) – *kholnu*
opinion – *raaya*
or – *ki*
orange – *suntalaa*
orange colour – *suntalaa rang*
ornament – *gahanaa*
other – *arko, aru*
otherwise – *natra*
out, outside – *baahira*
over – *maathi*
over there – *u tyahaā*

owl – *ullu*
ox – *goru*
oxygen – *praanbaayu*

P

packet – *poko, battaa*
pagoda – *gaajur*
pain – *dukhaai*
pain, hurt (v) – *dukhnu*
(a) pair – *jor*
painting – *chitra, thangka*
palace – *darbaar*
pale – *phikkaa*
papaya – *mewaa*
paper – *kaagaj*
parcel – *pulindaa*
pardon? – *hajur?*
parrot – *sugaa*
participate – *bhaag linu*
particular – *bishes*
party – *utsav*
pass – *bhanjyaang*
passenger – *yaatri*
passport – *raahadaani*
past (time) – *bhutkaal*
pasture – *kharka*
pay (v) – *tirnu*
peace – *shaanti*
peach – *aaru*
peacock – *mayur*
peak – *chuchuro*

peanut – *badaam*
pear – *naaspaati*
peas – *keraau*
pedestrian – *paidal yaatri*
pen – *kalam*
pencil – *sisaakalam*
people – *maanccheharu, janataa*
pepper – *marich*
percent – *pratishat*
permit (v) – *anumati dinu*
person – *maanchhe*
pet – *paaltu janaawar*
pharmacy – *ausadhi pasal*
pheasant – *kaalij*
phone (v) – *phon garnu*
photo – *tasbir*
photography – *tasbir khichne kalaa*
pick up (v) – *lina aaunu*
pickle – *achaar*
piece – *tukraa*
pig – *sūgur*
pigeon – *parewaa*
pillow – *siraani*
pineapple – *bhuīkatahar*
pink – *gulaaphi*
pipe – *churot paip*
place – *thaaū*
plains – *mades, taraai*
plainsdweller – *madesi*
plant – *biruwaa*

plate – *thaal*
platform (for cremation) – *ghat*
play (v) – *khelnu*
plum – *aarubakhadaa*
police – *prahari*
politics – *raajniti*
pomegranate – *anaar*
pond, tank – *pokhari*
poor – *garib*
pork – *sūgurko maasu*
porter – *bhariyaa*
post office – *hulaak addaa*
potato – *aalu*
pottery – *maatoko saamaan*
poverty – *daridrataa*
power – *shakti*
prayer – *puja, mantra, praarthanaa*

pregnant – *dojiyaa*
present (time) – *bartamaan samaya*
pressure – *thichaai, dabaad*
price – *mol*
pride – *garba*
priest – *paadari, pujaari*
private – *niji*
problem – *samasyaa*
proprietor (m) – *saahuji*
  (f) – *saahuni*
prostitute – *beshyaa*
protect – *bachaaunu*
protest – *birodh*
public – *saarbajanik*
purple – *pyaaji*
put – *raakhnu*
put into – *haalnu*

Q

queen – *raani*
question – *prashna*
quiet – *shaanta*
quietly – *bistaarai*
quilt – *sirak*

R

rabbit – *kharaayo*
race – sport – *daud*
  – people – *jaati*

radish – *mulaa*
rain (v) – *paani parnu*
rainy season – *barsaayaam*
raisin – *daakh*
rape (v) – *balaatkaar garnu*
rare – *durlabh*
rat – *musaa*
raw – *kaacho*
razorblade – *patti*
read (v) – *padhnu*
ready – *tayaar*
receipt – *bil*
recently – *haalsaalai*
recover (v) – *niko hunu*
red – *raato*
refuse (v) – *aswikaar garnu*
region – *kshetra*
relax – *aaraam garnu*
religion – *dharma*
remaining – *baaki*
remember – *samjhanu*
remote – *durgam*
repair (v) – *marmat garnu*
request – *anurodh*
respect (v) – *maannu*
rest (v) – *aaraam linu*
restaurant – *bhojanaalaya*
resting place – *chautaara*
return (v) – *pharkanu*
rhinoceros – *gaidaa*
rhododendron – *laali guraas*
rib – *karang*

rice – unhusked – *dhaan*
    – uncooked – *chaamal*
    – cooked – *bhaat*
rich – **dhani**
rickshaw – *rikshaa*
right – *daayaã*
ring – *aũthi*
ripe – *paakeko*
river – *nadi*
road, route – *baato*
rock – *paharo*
room – *kothaa*
rooster – *bhaale*
rope – **dori**
rough – *khasro*
round – **dallo**
rub (v) – *dalnu*
rupees – *rupaiyaã*

S

sad/sorry – *dukha*
safe – *surakshit*
safety pin – *huk*
saffron – *keshar*
saint – *mahaatmaa*
salt – *nun*
salty – *nunilo*
sandal – *chappal*
sari – *saari*
Saturday – *sanibaar*
say (v) – *bhannu*

scared – **dar**
scenery – *drishya*
school – *paathshaalaa*
scientist – *baigyaanik*
scissors – *kaĩchi*
seated (to be) – *basi raakhnu*
secret – *gopya*
secretary – *sachib*
see (v) – *hernu, dekhnu*
seed – *biu*
self – *aaphno*
sell – *bechnu*
send – *pathaaunu*
servant – *nokar*
serve – *sewaa sarnu*
sesame seed – *tilko biu*
sew – *siunu*
shade – *shital*
shampoo – *dhulaai*
share (v) – *baãdnu*
shave – *khauranu*
shawl – *o**d**ne*
she – informal – *u, tyo, yo*
    – formal – *wahaã*
sheep – *bhe**d**o*
sheet – *tannaa*
shelter – *baas*
shirt – *kamij*
shiver (v) – *kaamnu*
shoe – *juttaa*
shop – *pasal*
shopkeeper – *pasale, saahu*

shopping – *kinmel*
short – *chhoto*
shorts – *kattu*
shoulder – *kaādh*
shout (v) – *chichyaaunu*
show (v) – *dekhaaunu*
shower (v) – *nuhaaunu*
shyness – *laaj*
sick – *biraami*
sickness – *rog*
side – *patti, chheu*
(this) side – *waari*
(that) side – *paari*
silence – *maunataa*
silk – *resham*
silver – *chaādi*
simple – *sajilo*
sin – *paap*
sing – *gaaunu*
single man
  (unmarried) – *kumaar*
single woman
  (unmarried) – *kumaari*
sister – elder – *didi*
  – younger – *bahini*
sisters – *didbahini*
sitting posture – *asana*
skin – *chhaalaa*
sky – *aakaash*
sleep (v) – *sutnu*
sleeping bag – *sutne jholaa*
sleepy – *nidraa*

slow – **dhilo**
slowly – *bistaarai*
small – *saano*
small change – *khudraa paisaa*
smell bad (v) – *ganaaunu*
smile (v) – *muskaaunu*
smoke (v) – *(churot)khaanu*
smoking – *dhumrapaan*
snack – *khaajaa*
snake – *saāp*
snow – *hiū*
soap – *saabun*
sock – *mojaa*
soil – *maato*
soldier – *sipaahi*
some – *kehi, kunai*
someone – *kohi*
something – *kehi*
sometimes – *kahile kahi*
son – *chhoraa*
soon – *chaādai*
sore – *dukheko*
soul, spirit – *aatmaa*
soup – *jhol*
sour – *amilo*
south – *dakshin*
soybeans – *bhatmaas*
speak (v) – *bolnu*
spend – *kharcha garnu*
spice – *masalaa*
spicy – *piro*

spider – *maakura*
spinach – *paalungo*
spoon – *chamchaa*
sport – *khelkud*
sprain – *markaai*
spring – *basanta ritu*
squash – *iskus, laukaa,
    ghiraŭlo*
squirrel – *lokharke*
stale – *baasi*
stamp – *tikat*
stand (v) – *ubhinu*
standing (to be) – *uthi
    raakhnu*
stationery – *chitthipatralaai
    chaahine saamaan*
statue – *murti*
stay/sit (v) – *basnu*
steal (v) – *chornu*
steep – uphill – *thado*
    – downhill – *bhiraalo,
    paharilo*
stick – *latthi*
stomach – *pet*
stone – *dhungaa*
stop (v) – *roknu*
storm – *huri*
story – *kathaa*
stove – *chulo*
straight – *sidhaa, sojho*
strike, ring (v) – *bajnu*
string – *dori*

strong – *baliyo*
student – *bidyaarthi*
stupid – *murka*
sugar – *chini*
sugar cane – *ukhu*
suitcase – *sutkes*
summer – *garmi mausam*
Sunday – *aitbaar*
sunny – *ghamailo*
sure – *pakkaa*
surprise – *chhakka*
sweet – *guliyo*
sweet lime – *mosam*
sweet potato – *sakhaarkhanda*
swim (v) – *paudi khelnu*

T

table – *tebul*
tail – *puchchhar*
tailor – *darji*
take (v) – *linu*
take away (v) – *laanu*
take a photo – *tasbir khichnu*
talcum – *abhrakh*
tall – *aglo*
tamarind – *amili*
tasty – *mitho*
taxi – *tyaaksi*
tea – *chiyaa*
teacher – *shikshak*
telephone – *teliphon*

telephone (v) – *phon garnu*
tell (v) – *bhannu*
temperature – *taapkram*
temple (Hindu) – *mandir*
　　(Buddhist) – *stupa*
tent – *paal*
test – *jaāch*
tetanus – *dhanurog*
than – *bhandaa*
thank you – *dhanyabaad*
that – *tyo*
there – *tyahaā*
these – *yi*
they – formal – *uniharu*
　　– informal – *wahaāharu*
thief – *chor*
thin – *paatalo, dublo*
thing – material – *chij*
　　– abstract – *kuraa*
things – *chijbij*
think (v) – *bichaar garnu*
third – *tihaai*
thirst/thirsty – *tirkhaa*
this – *yo*
those – *ti*
thread – *dhaago*
throat – *ghaāti*
thunder – *garjan*
thunderstorm – *meghgarjan*
　　tathaa barsaa
Thursday – *bihibaar*
Tibetan dress – *chubaa*

tick – *kirno*
ticket – **tikat**
tiger – *baagh*
tighten (v) – *kasinu*
time – *samay, pa**t**ak*
timetable – *samaya taalikaa*
tip – *bakas*
tired – *thakaai, thakyo*
to – *laai*
tobacco – *surti*
today – *aaja*
toilet – *charpi*
tomato – *golbhē**d**a*
tomorrow – *bholi*
tongue – *jibro*
tonight – *aaja raati*
too – *dherai, saahrai*
tooth – *daāt*
toothbrush – *daāt maajhne*
　　burus
toothpick – *sinko*
total – *jammaa*
tour, walk, turn (v) – *ghumnu*
tourism – *parya**t**an*
tourist – *parya**t**ak*
tourist office – *parya**t**an*
　　kaaryaalaya
towards – *tira*
towel – *rumaal*
town – *nagar*
trader – *saahu*
trail – *saano baa**t**o*

travel (v) – *yaatraa garnu*
traveller – *batuwaa*
tree – *rukh*
trip – *yaatraa*
trousers – *suruwaal*
try (v) – *kosis garnu*
try on – *lagaai hernu*
T-shirt – *ganji*
Tuesday – *mangalbaar*
tunic – *daauraa*
turmeric – *besaar*
turn (v) – *mo**d**nu*
turnip – *salgam*
type – *kisim*
typhoid – ***taiphaaid***

U

umbrella – *chhaataa*
under – *muni*
underpants – *kattu*
understand – *bujhnu*
undress – *phukaalnu*
university – *bishwabi dyaalaya*
unripe – *kaācho*
until/up to – *samma*
up – *maathi*
up there – *u maathi*
uphill – *ukaalo*
upward – *maastira*
urinate (v) – *pisaab garnu*

urine – *pisaab*
useful – *kaamlaagne*
useless – *binaakaamko*
utensil – *bhaā**d**aa*

V

vaccination – *sui*
valley – *upatyakaa*
valuable – *bahumulya*
vegetables – *tarkaari*
vegetarian – *saakaahaari*
vehicle – *gaa**d**i*
venereal disease – *bhiringi*
very – *dherai, ekdam*
vest – *ganji*
view – *drishya*
village – *gaaū*
vinegar – *sirkhaa*
visa – *bhija*
vitamin – *bhitaamin*
voice – *swar*
volume – *maanaa*
vomit (v) – *baantaa garnu*
vote (v) – *mat khasaalnu*
vulture – *giddha*

W

waistcoat – *istakot*
wait (v) – *parkhanu*
waiter – *beraa*

walk (v) – *hĩdnu*
walnut – *okhar*
want (v) – *chaahanu*
warm – *nyaano*
wash (v) – people – *nuhaaunu*
– things – *dhunu*
watch – *ghadi*
watch (v) – *hernu*
water – *paani*
– boiled – *umaaleko paani*
waterfall – *jharnaa*
way – *baato*
we – *haami(haru)*
weak – *kamjor*
weather – *mausam*
Wednesday – *budhbaar*
wedding – *bihaa*
week – *haptaa*
weekly market – *haat bajaar*
welcome (v) – *swaagat garnu*
well – *sanchai, aaraamai*
west – *pashchim*
wet – *bhijeko*
what – *ke*
wheat – *gahũ*
when – *kahile*
where – *kahaã*
which – *kun*
white – *seto*
who – *ko*
whole – *jammai*
whose – *kasko*

why – *kina*
wide – *pharaakilo*
wife – own – *swaasni*
– someone else's – *srimati*
will be – *holaa*
wind – *haawaa*
window – *jhyaal*
windy – *haawaa laagne*
winter – *jaado mahinaa*
wise – *buddhimaan*
with – *sãga, sita, le*
without – *bina*
woman – *aaimaai*
wood – *kaath*
wooden article – *kaathbaata baneko bastu*
wool – *un*
work – *kaam*
worker – *majdur*
world – *samsaar*
worried – *pir*
worship – *pujaa*
write (v) – *lekhnu*
writer – *lekhak*
writing paper – *lekhne kaapi*
wrong – *bethik, galat*

Y

yak – *chaũrigaai*
yak meat – *chaũrigaaiko maasu*

yam – *tarul*
year – *barsa, sal*
yellow – *pahēlo*
yes – *ā, ho, chha, hunchha, achchhaa*
yesterday – *hijo*
yeti – *yeti*
yoga – *yog*
yoghurt – *dahi*

you (sg) – informal – *timi*
  – formal – *tapaaī*
(pl) – informal – *timiharu*
  – formal – *tapaaīharu*
young – *jawaan*

Z

zone – *anchal*
zoo – *chidiyaakhaanaa*

Emergencies

Help!	*guhaar!*
Thief!	*chor!*
Watch out!	*hera!*
Go away!	*jaau!*

I've been robbed.	*chorle malaai lutyo*
They took my ...	*usle mero ... choryo*
I've lost my ...	*mero ... haraayo*
bag/backpack	*jholaa, thailo*
camera	*kyaameraa*
money	*paisaa*
passport	*raahadaani*

It's an emergency!	*aapat bhayo!*
There's been an accident!	*durghatanaa bhayo!*
Please call a doctor.	*daaktarlaai bolaaunuhos*
We need transport.	*haamilaai yaataayaat chaahiyo*

I have/He/She has altitude sickness.	*malaai/tyaslaai uchchaai laagyo*
I am ill.	*ma biraami chhu*
I want to go to ...	*ma ... jaanchhu*

On the trekking circuits, there are small hospitals in Jiri, Phaphlu and Khunde (near Namche Bazaar), while the Himalayan Rescue Association has a medical facility in Pheriche, on the Everest Trek, and the Edmund Hilary Hospital is at Khumjung. On the Annapurna Circuit, go to Manang.

141

I am lost.	*ma haraẽ*
I've been raped.	*malaai balaatkaar garyo*
Could you help me, please?	*malaai maddat garna saknuhunchha?*
Where is the toilet?	*charpi kahaã chha?*
I'm sorry/I apologise.	*malaai maph garnuhos*
I didn't realise I was doing anything wrong.	*malaai thaahaa bhaena galti bhayo*
I didn't do it.	*maile garinã*
Could I please use the telephone?	*ma telephon garna sakinchha?*
I wish to contact my enbassy/consulate.	*ma raajdutaavaasmaa samparka garnu parchha*

Nepal
a travel survival kit
**Tony Wheeler &
Richard Everist**

Travel information on every road-accessible area in Nepal, including the Terai. This practical guidebook also includes introductions to trekking, white-water rafting and mountain biking.

Trekking in the Nepal Himalaya
Stan Armington

Complete trekking information for Nepal, including day-by-day route descriptions and detailed maps – a wealth of advice for both independent and group trekkers.

Where Can You Find Out........

HOW to get a Laotian visa in Bangkok?
WHERE to go birdwatching in PNG?
WHAT to expect from the police if you're robbed in Peru?
WHEN you can go to see cow races in Australia?

In the Lonely Planet Newsletter!

Every issue includes:

- a letter from Lonely Planet founders Tony and Maureen Wheeler
- a letter from an author 'on the road'
- the most entertaining or informative reader's letter we've received
- the latest news on new and forthcoming releases from Lonely Planet
- and all the latest travel news from all over the world

To receive the FREE quarterly Lonely Planet Newsletter, write to:
Lonely Planet Publications Pty Ltd (A.C.N. 005 607 983)
PO Box 617, Hawthorn, Vic 3122, Australia
Lonely Planet Publications, Inc
PO Box 2001A, Berkeley, CA 94702, USA